Enchantment of the World

BULGARIA

By Abraham Resnick

Consultant for Bulgaria: Howard I. Aronson, Ph.D., Professor, Department of Slavic Languages and Literature, The University of Chicago, Chicago, Illinois

Consultant for Reading: Robert L. Hillerich, Ph.D., Professor Emeritus, Bowling Green State University; Consultant, Pinellas County Schools, Florida

CP CHILDRENS PRESS ®
CHICAGO

For the National Festival of Folk Dances and Songs at Koprivshtitsa, women dress in traditional folk costumes.

Project Editor: Mary Reidy
Design: Margrit Fiddle
Photo Research: Judy Feldmen

Library of Congress Cataloging-in-Publication Data

Resnick, Abraham.
  Bulgaria / by Abraham Resnick.
    p.   cm. – (Enchantment of the world)
  Includes index.
  Summary: Discusses the geography, history, people, economy, and customs of this Balkan country.
  ISBN 0-516-02631-3
  1. Bulgaria–Juvenile literature. [1. Bulgaria.]
I. Title. II. Series.
DR67.7.R47 1995   94-37948
949.77–dc20   CIP
                                                        AC

Picture Acknowledgments
AP/Wide World Photos: 30 (right), 34, 36, 40, 57, 72 (left)
The Bettmann Archive: 24, 31
North Wind Picture Archives: 29, 30 (left)
Photri: 12, 71, 90, 92, 93 (right), 94, 95 (left), 97; © **D. J. Dianellis,** 8, 48 (left)
Abraham Resnick: Cover, Cover Inset, 6, 9, 11, 17 (2 photos), 21, 45 (2 photos), 46, 51, 53 (3 photos), 59 (2 photos), 60 (left), 61 (2 photos), 68, 69, 71 (left), 73 (left), 74 (4 photos), 79 (right), 80, 83, 85, 86, 95 (right), 96, 98 (2 photos), 104, 121; © **Abraham Resnick:** 51 (right), 51 (inset), 60 (right), 63 (right), 86 (inset), 103 (left)
Reuters/Bettmann: 37, 38 (2 photos), 72 (right), 79 (left)
Stock Montage: 18
Tony Stone Images: © **Sylvain Grandadam,** 64, 76 (right), 83 (bottom inset); © **Rosemary Evans,** 83 (top inset), 100, 101, 103 (right), 104 (inset)
SuperStock International, Inc.: © **Kurt Scholz,** 67 (right), 73 (right), 91; © **Gerard F. Fritz,** 89
UPI/Bettmann: 32 (2 photos), 35
Viesti Associates, Inc.: © **Joe Viesti,** 4, 48 (right), 54 (2 photos), 63 (left), 66, 67 (left), 70, 76 (left), 93 (left), 114-115, 122
Visuals Unlimited: © **McCutcheon,** 10
Len W. Meents: Maps on 81, 85, 100, 103
Courtesy Flag Research Center, Winchester, Massachusetts 01890: Flag on back cover
Cover: Ski resort of Mt. Vitosha, near Sofia
Cover Inset: Sunflower field

*Traditional
costumes worn
at Sofia's
Spring Festival*

TABLE OF CONTENTS

A village in the Balkan Mountains

Chapter 1

BORDERS AND
BOUNDARIES

Bulgaria, with its pivotal location in the Balkan Peninsula in southeastern Europe, is situated at the center of cultural crossroads, where civilizations of the East and West have met and merged. Because of Bulgaria's location in the Balkans, with their long, troublesome history of warfare, Bulgaria's ways of living, past and present, have been greatly influenced by invading forces. The cultural pattern of Bulgaria reflects Slavic, Byzantine, Roman, Ottoman (Turkish), and western European characteristics. The lower Danube River serves as a boundary with Romania on the north; Serbia and the Republic of Macedonia, which were both part of the old Yugoslavia, lie to the west; and Greece and Turkey extend along Bulgaria's southern edge. In the south the border with Greece passes through hills and mountains, and the boundary separating Bulgaria and Turkey cuts across the Thracian Plain, a broad flat area in the southeast.

In the past Bulgaria fell prey to ruthless raiders, brutal invaders, and conquering armies. For five hundred years, starting in 1396, Bulgaria was controlled by the Turks and endured oppression and suffering.

A monument in Sofia commemorates the liberation of Bulgaria from the Nazis by the Soviet Army.

Bulgaria's location and geography have had positive dimensions too. Greece and, especially, Turkey have had considerable influence on Bulgarian architecture, cuisine, customs, and to a lesser degree, on its fine tradition of art, music, and dance.

But the country that during the twentieth century has had the closest association with Bulgaria isn't even a neighbor. It is Russia, part of the former Soviet Union, located at least 500 miles (805 kilometers) away from the Bulgarian border. Since the 1870s, when Russia helped liberate Bulgaria from the grip of the Ottoman Turks, relations between the two countries have been quite friendly. Both Russians and Bulgarians speak Slavic languages and many people from both countries practice the Eastern Orthodox religion. In 1944 during World War II, the Soviet army helped rid Bulgaria of Nazi troops and pro-Nazi collaborators.

Duni resort, near Sozopol, is a large, modern seaside facility with fishing, boating, swimming, and entertainment.

THE BLACK SEA

In the east, Bulgaria has a 175-mile (282-kilometer) coastline along the Black Sea, which throughout history has proved to be both friend and foe to those who have sailed its waters. Legend has it that the Black Sea received its name from the blackish appearance of the clouds and water during severe winter storms or because fog lying over the sea in winter makes the water appear black.

Over the centuries many fishers have drowned in the Black Sea. Sailors became superstitious about venturing out on its fogbound waters. But today more than 1.5 million people vacation at the Black Sea coast each year. They come for the abundance of sunshine, delightful sea breezes, and ideal temperatures. Hundreds of fine resort complexes provide just about every kind of leisure-

9

The Danube River forms part of the Bulgarian-Romanian border.

time activity imaginable. Most resorts are set along excellent sandy beaches or on wooded hills overlooking scenic bays and tideless inlets. And the clear blue waters are always inviting.

Perhaps the Black Sea, at least off the coast of Bulgaria, has been misnamed. Some believe that the name "Bright Sea" would be much more appropriate.

PHYSICAL FEATURES

Bulgaria is rather small in size, only about as large as the state of Tennessee or the Central American country of Guatemala. Its greatest distance from east to west is 306 miles (492 kilometers). The Danube River forms most of the Romanian-Bulgarian border in the north. A large part of Bulgaria's northern region, 28 percent, consists of the Danubian Plain. Another plain, the Thracian Plain in the south, is easily identified. Bulgaria's most important river, the Maritsa, flows through the plain. No rivers within the country are navigable.

Skiers in the Rhodope Mountains

Two great mountain ranges, the Balkan (*Balkan* is a Turkish word meaning "mountain") in the center of the country and the Rhodope in the south and southwest, are joined together near Sofia, the capital of Bulgaria, at the foot of another important mountain, Vitosha.

From the air these east-west mountains take on a wishbone appearance. The Rhodope Mountains include the Rila and Pirin ranges, which contain the highest mountains in the Balkan Peninsula. The country's highest point, Musala Peak, rises 9,596

feet (2,925 meters) above sea level. Peaks in the Balkan Mountains range from 3,500 to 7,800 feet (1,067 to 2,377 meters) in elevation.

In addition to Bulgaria's broken, mountainous terrain—which totals about 40 percent of the country's natural topography—there is a great diversity in landforms throughout the country. The greater part of the Bulgarian territory, however, is occupied by flat, slightly hilly land.

Bulgaria's best soil is found on the Danubian Plain. The fertile farmland of the region produces grains, mostly wheat and corn, and industrial crops such as sunflowers, sugar beets, and tobacco. Several Bulgarian rivers, including the Iskur and the Yantra, flow northward on the plain into the Danube.

Bulgaria's Thracian Plain is also a productive agricultural region. The irrigated fields are primarily known for their fruits, vegetables, and vineyards.

The Balkan Mountains offer rich forests. Where erosion has taken place the mountains and hills are being reforested. For the most part the mountains are composed of hard granite and crystalline rocks. The region provides some coal and deposits of copper, lead, iron ore, zinc, gold, and fireclay, clay that can be baked at high temperatures.

The Rhodope Mountains consist mainly of granite and limestone. Here are found rich stores of timber, chiefly beech, oak, and pine. An assortment of ores and minerals are extracted from the mountains: lead, zinc, chrome, copper, coal, and volcanic rocks used for making cement and plaster compounds. However, the country's mineral and raw material resources are limited.

WILDLIFE

Over the years an array of wildlife roamed the hills and mountains of Bulgaria. Even the legendary lion once made his home in the dens and caves of the Bulgarian uplands. Later the lion became a cherished emblem that appears on the Bulgarian coat of arms.

As human activity and hunting increased and forests were cut down in or near the animal domains, the threat of attacks by wildlife diminished. Bulgarian folktales for children frequently recount the lore of shepherds who used cunning to "outfox" predatory animals descending the hills in quest of sheep and goats grazing in the pastures below. Many Bulgarian stories tell of the heroics of villagers who embarked on nighttime expeditions to hunt down and destroy packs of wolves about to advance on their hamlets in search of food.

VARIATIONS IN CLIMATE

The north and northwest sections of Bulgaria have a moderately continental climate. Summers are warm to cool, winters are cold, and there is moderate precipitation year-round. These areas are influenced by air masses that flow over a large expanse of land before reaching Bulgaria. In fact, the Danube River has been known to freeze over when cold winter air flows southward. Yet summer temperatures and humidity can be quite high in northern Bulgaria.

Farther south, in the west, southwest, and central sections of the country, the temperatures become somewhat more moderate and not unlike the weather conditions found in southern California. Actually parts of the Black Sea coast resemble the Mediterranean climate, where the winters are mild and rainy and summers hot and dry.

The Mesta and Struma River Valleys and the southeast also take on the characteristics of the Mediterranean climate, often with summer drought. Here the summers are warm, and occasionally rather hot, while the winters are fairly cold. Finally, in the higher sections of the country, like Sofia, which is 1,805 feet (550 meters) above sea level, and other elevations higher than 3,000 feet (914 meters), the typical temperatures are cold in winter and quite pleasant during the summer months.

The sun shines in Bulgaria from an average of about two hours a day in January to an average of ten hours a day in midsummer. The average yearly precipitation is 25 inches (64 centimeters). However, mountainous areas usually receive more than 40 inches (102 centimeters), but much of that amount is in the form of snow. The snow may lie on the highest mountains until June. But snowfall is generally light elsewhere in the nation.

Although the climate in Bulgaria is primarily temperate, its variability throughout the year means that it may be uncomfortably cold in winter and rather warm and sultry in summer. Spring can be ideal but changeable, and the fall is pleasant, but these seasons in Bulgaria experience sudden changes between warm and cold days.

Chapter 2

MUSEUMS, MONUMENTS, AND MEMORIES

The Bulgarian people have a deep sense of history. Hardly a town or city is without a statue, monument, museum, historical marker, or commemorative house. Every effort is made to keep alive the memory of those who made special contributions to Bulgaria's past, be they poet or peasant, soldier or patriot. Tributes to those who have fallen in uprisings and battles seem to be everywhere. Throughout the land many churches and monasteries display age-old artistry that attests to Bulgaria's long record of cultural achievements.

Today there are more than thirty thousand archaeological, architectural, historical, and artistic monuments in Bulgaria, some in recognition of the ancient cultures that flourished on its territory. In Sofia there are more than 250 historic monuments. Bulgaria is considered to be one of the oldest settled lands in all of Europe. In 1981 it marked its thirteen hundredth birthday as a nation.

ANCIENT INHABITANTS

Archaeological diggings have unearthed some astonishing findings in various parts of Bulgaria. In and around Veliko Turnovo traces of the existence of primitive people—actual cave dwellers—have been found. At that time, 50,000 to 100,000 years ago, Bulgaria was covered with ice and glaciers dominated the mountains. But lower places were habitable. There is evidence that there was human settlement in Bulgaria many thousands of years before the Stone Age.

The earliest people of the region were familiar with fire. Living in tribal communities, they relied on hunting, fishing, and the gathering of herbs and roots for their survival. Their tools and weapons were shaped from stone. Bone was used for making needles, fishhooks, and knives. Clothes were made of unprocessed hides.

In later ages people began to live on the open plains as the climate became milder and the ice fields melted. These people began to use more sophisticated implements and utensils. Some found in Varna and the town of Stara Zagora are dated from about 1,000 B.C. Burial mounds discovered in Bulgaria show that life in some settlements went on for twelve hundred years. Excavations in Sofia have proved that it is one of the oldest inhabited places in the world. It was first settled some seven thousand years ago, and Plovdiv, Bulgaria's second-largest city, located at the center of the Thracian Plain, had people living there five thousand years ago. In antiquity the Bulgarian lands were populated by the Thracians. They established the first civilization in Bulgaria in the Bronze Age, more than four thousand years before the birth of Christ.

Sculptures from a tomb (left) and silver vessels (right) show the skills of the Thracian artists and craftspeople.

The Thracians were a highly advanced people, making exceptional ornaments and idols of bone and marble. Much was learned about their lives from their burial grounds scattered over Bulgaria. The Thracians believed in life after death. A dead man was buried with a favorite wife, his horses hitched to his battle chariot, and various weapons and utensils.

The Thracians were known to be gifted singers, musicians, and dancers. They also were excellent farmers, craftspeople, and merchants. They adopted the Greek alphabet and culture and built up a line of trade with their Greek neighbor to the south. In the fourth century B.C. Alexander the Great conquered Thrace and the entire Balkan area. Then by the middle of the second century B.C., new conquerors, the Roman legions, invaded the region and subjected all the people living there to Roman domination. Most of the population was forced into slavery and had to do hard labor on the newly established large estates and in quarries and workshops. Many Thracian slaves were forced to serve in distant

Khan Krum ruled in the beginning of the ninth century.

parts of the Roman Empire. The strongest and bravest in their ranks were carted off to Rome. There they became gladiators, forced to fight for their lives against other men and ferocious animals in arenas packed with taunting spectators.

FOUNDATIONS FROM THE MIDDLE AGES

Once the power of the Romans diminished in the Balkan Peninsula, two separate groups of people migrated into the region. Slavic people moved southward from locations that are now part of Ukraine and Belorussia. Then around A.D. 600, a small group of Turkic nomads from the area north of the Caspian Sea found their way into the territory around the mouth of the Danube and along the Black Sea coast. They were known as Bulgars. The Slavs and the Bulgars intermarried and became the forerunners of present-day Bulgarians.

The first Bulgarian kingdom was established in A.D. 681. It had a feudal society with power in the hands of the nobles. The early rulers had the title of khan, a title reserved for lords and princes who dominated most of Asia and southeast Europe during the Middle Ages. The lowly peasants worked the land and the resources of the region began to be developed under Khan Krum and later Khan Omurtag, rulers of the Bulgarian kingdom in the beginning of the ninth century. Written laws were introduced and Bulgaria became a united nation with equality shared by both Slav and Bulgar elements. The country became centralized with power and authority in one organization, palaces were built, and many construction projects were begun.

This period of history was marked by years of brutal warfare between the Bulgarians and the Byzantines (Greeks). On one occasion the Bulgarian troops reached the walls of Constantinople, now known as Istanbul, in Turkey. Armies were used to gain control of territories or to rob the enemy. In one battle Khan Krum's troops seized a Byzantine convoy carrying 1,100 pounds (499 kilograms) of gold.

CHRISTIANITY ADOPTED

In time a peace treaty with Byzantium was signed. Under Boris I, who demanded to be called *tsar,* or "emperor," Christianity was adopted in 865, and Boris himself was baptized along with his family. Those who did not agree with this act mutinied against Boris, and he quickly sentenced the rebels and their families to death. With the coming of Christianity to Bulgaria, the people could now identify with a common religion, and Bulgaria no longer was considered a barbarian state. Differences between Bulgarians tended to decrease, and the nation was able to build closer ties with more culturally advanced European countries.

The golden age of Bulgarian culture under the reign of Tsar

Simeon, beginning in 893, laid the foundation for further intellectual advancement. Bulgaria created its own literature and art. New ideas were brought into the country by priests and scholars from other countries.

Simeon, who was educated in Constantinople, is generally considered the greatest of all Bulgarian rulers. He came to power in a most unusual way. After Boris introduced Christianity to Bulgaria, Boris was ordained a monk and entered a monastery, handing over the throne to his son Vladimir. But Vladimir denounced Christianity and attempted to restore the old pagan ways. This made Boris angry. Feeling betrayed, Boris left the monastery, captured and blinded his son, and installed his other son, Simeon, on the throne.

Tsar Simeon chose the Eastern Orthodox religion for Bulgaria. He looked to the patriarch of Constantinople rather than the pope in Rome for guidance. Moreover, he thought that the Eastern Orthodox church would enable Bulgaria to have more of a national church, less subject to outside influences.

CYRIL AND METHODIUS

A new Slav-Christian society began during the late ninth and early tenth centuries, based on the Slavic alphabet that was used to write the Bible and certain prayers. It is believed that the alphabet was devised by a monk, Cyril, with the help of his brother Methodius, also a monk. Cyril was considered to be one of the best-educated clergymen of his time. Both men knew Greek and Slavic from their childhood. They were sent in 862 by the Byzantine emperor to a place called "Greater Moravia" (generally believed to be in the present-day Czech Republic), where they

A fresco shows Cyril and Methodius, the creators of the Slavic alphabet.

created in the following year a unique alphabet for the Slavic language. This alphabet is known as *Glagolitic*. The mission to Moravia was ended by local German bishops, and many of the followers of Cyril and Methodius went to Bulgaria, where there soon arose a *new* Slavic alphabet, based mainly on the Greek alphabet. This alphabet is called the *Cyrillic* and is in use among all Eastern Orthodox Slavs as well as a number of non-Slavic people in the republics of former Soviet Central Asia and Caucasia.

THE BYZANTINE EMPIRE

After Simeon's death in 927, Bulgarian power declined rapidly. The frequent wars with the Byzantines and Bulgaria's neighbors to the north took their toll on the people and the resources of the country. The Byzantine Empire, on the other hand, strengthened its position in the Balkans. It was easy to conquer the eastern part of Bulgaria. In 1014 a new Bulgarian tsar, Samuel, tried to win back lost territory, but was soundly defeated by the Byzantine emperor Basil II, nicknamed "the Bulgarian killer."

Basil lived up to his reputation in one of the most infamous battles of all time. After fourteen thousand Bulgarians were taken prisoner, Basil ordered ninety-nine of each one hundred captives to be blinded so that they could never fight again. When they returned home, Tsar Samuel, on seeing what had been done to his soldiers, suffered a heart attack and died two days later.

From 1018 to 1185 the country came under the domination of the Byzantine Empire. With the weakening of Bulgaria, the lower classes became tired of long years of warfare. There was a growing trend to preach pacifism, equality, and disobedience to authority. Many people turned against the tsar, the noblemen, and the clergy, who had been living luxurious lives at the expense of the poor. The people especially denounced the symbols and rituals of the church and materialism. A number of people lived in communes, and some even became spiritual hermits and heretics. This movement, called *Bogomilism*, was to make Bulgaria weak from within. Bogomils were followers of a medieval religious sect that originated in the eighth century in Bulgaria. The movement was probably started by a priest named *Bogomil*, a Slavic word meaning "pleasing to God." The Bogomilist movement was a mixture of local, mostly Christian elements that sought reforms in the Bulgarian Orthodox church.

Bogomils believed that the visible world was created by the devil and that the soul alone was God's creation, and therefore was good. Their leaders, called "perfects," abstained from sexual relations, alcohol, and meat. Ordinary believers led less strict lives. They rejected the hierarchy and sacraments of the Orthodox church until their dying hours.

During the eleventh and twelfth centuries Bogomilism spread over European and Asian provinces of the Byzantine Empire. The Bogomils were respected everywhere for their moral values, but they were persecuted wherever they went. In Bulgaria, Bogomilism remained a powerful force until the fourteenth century. The movement spread through the Balkans and finally reached France, where its practitioners were called Catharis or Albigensians. Some branches of the sect were able to persuade others to denounce unjust authoritarian rule and to embrace Bogomilist precepts and practices.

A major center for the Bogomils was located in Bosnia, where some may have accepted Islam after the advance of the Turks in 1453. Today Slavic-speaking Muslims are found in Bosnia, Bulgaria, and throughout the Balkans.

THE BEGINNING OF ISLAM

Before the establishment of the first Bulgarian kingdom, the Prophet Muhammad was born in Mecca in what is now Saudi Arabia. Muhammad founded the religion of Islam, whose followers are called Muslims. By the year A.D. 732, one hundred years after Muhammad's death, the Muslims controlled the Middle East, including places sacred to Christianity such as Jerusalem. Their rule extended to Spain, North Africa, and much of the Byzantine Empire.

SECOND BULGARIAN KINGDOM

At the end of the twelfth century, Byzantine rule of Bulgaria began to weaken. Constant attacks by foreign armies and rebel

An engraving of the city of Veliko Turnovo,
which was established in the Middle Ages.

forces within Bulgaria took their toll and eroded the power of Byzantine warlords. Also at this time Constantinople and its army had to contend with the Third Crusade. The crusade consisted of an army of Christians determined to recover the Holy Land from the Muslims. Conditions were ripe for someone to lead a revolt against the Byzantine state.

Ivan and Peter Asen came from a landowning family named Belgun. They led a popular uprising to become independent of Constantinople. The second Bulgarian kingdom was proclaimed in 1186. A peace treaty was concluded and a new capital was established in the city of Veliko Turnovo.

Not long after Ivan Asen took the title and role of tsar, he was murdered by a nobleman. The throne was taken by his brother Peter, who also was killed. Kaloyan then became tsar. He led the Bulgarian army on successful military expeditions at Varna, along the Black Sea, to the south in Thrace, and to the southwest in Macedonia. Kaloyan, who was a shrewd military strategist, was able to defeat the Magyars (the Hungarians) in the northwest. Bulgaria had become powerful again. Its boundary even extended as far west as Belgrade, in Serbia.

Tsar Kaloyan's reign was unusual because he established friendly relations with the pope in Rome. While leading a siege of Salonika in 1207, in what is now Greece, Kaloyan was killed. Kaloyan's killing was engineered by *bolyars*, members of the privileged aristocracy of Bulgaria. Boril, his nephew, was involved in the conspiracy against him. Boril immediately seized power, only to be deposed eleven years later.

Fortunately for Bulgaria, Ivan Asen II came to power in 1218. The new tsar was a just, wise, and moderate man—most unusual for rulers during the Middle Ages. He ruled for twenty-three years and proved to be the greatest of all Bulgarian rulers. Ivan allowed his authority to be shared. He decreed that the lands owned by monasteries could be farmed by free peasants. Commerce within the country expanded, and foreign sea trade extended all the way to Venice and Genoa in Italy. Coins were minted. Bulgarian history was written. Bulgaria prospered, and its architecture, religious literature, and the arts flourished. Many churches and monasteries were constructed. Veliko Turnovo, the capital, was expanded and enriched.

None of the successors of Ivan Asen II was able to maintain a strong central authority, and once again Bulgaria began to decay. Political disorder, violence, and lawlessness were repeated. Northern Bulgaria was ravaged by Mongols, people from Mongolia, north of China. Feudal leaders gained control over their own provinces, and Turks, Greeks, and Hungarians tried to form their own domains in the country. Assassinations were common. Dynasty followed dynasty, and all proved weak. Bulgaria was divided into two kingdoms and a new capital was established at Vidin, competing with the older capital at Veliko Turnovo.

External and internal wars further devastated the country. Bitter wars, with brother killing brother, led to a rapid weakening of Bulgaria. And the never-ending wars with its neighbors continued. A Bulgarian ruler, Michael III Shishman, a brother-in-law of the king of Serbia, desperately attacked his relative's army. Michael III was killed in battle in 1330. By the middle of the fourteenth century, the historical region known as Macedonia, located in the present-day Republic of Macedonia, northern Greece, and western Bulgaria, was under Serbian control, and Bulgaria came under strong Serbian influence. To make matters worse, the Ottoman Turks with their powerful armies began to penetrate into the Balkans and captured Sofia. In 1388, the Turks easily defeated the Serbs in battle. By 1396, all of Bulgaria was under Turkish domination, an occupation that was to last for 500 years. After 208 years, the second Bulgarian kingdom came to an end.

TURKISH RULE

Though the five-hundred-year domination of Bulgaria by the Ottomans was often harsh, not all Bulgarians experienced the same living conditions during the occupation of their land. In the first centuries of rule over Bulgaria, the Ottoman Empire was a well-organized, enlightened, and modern state for its time. A political system granting limited national and local autonomy was introduced. This enabled certain Bulgarians to manage their own affairs under Ottoman authority.

Under the Ottoman rule subjects were divided according to their religion. Bulgarians who accepted the Muslim faith were treated much better than Bulgarian Christians who remained loyal to their religion. Christians refusing to convert to Islam were considered inferior, and their rights and interests were subordinated to those granted Bulgarian Muslims. Though many Christians were forced to submit to humiliations in their personal lives by Ottoman overseers, lowly Bulgarian peasants working on estates found their status and lifestyle no worse under their new masters than it had been under Christian landlords. In some instances their political and social status was even better.

More and more Turks poured into Bulgaria. By the end of the sixteenth century, two-thirds of Sofia's population was Turkish. Bulgarian participation in trade was almost totally wiped out. Craftspeople produced little, economic life was at a standstill, and the Black Sea ports were closed to foreign vessels.

After the seventeenth century, the Ottoman Empire entered a period of slow decline. Trade routes were changing. Russia and Austria were becoming more powerful and started to expand their frontiers into lands dominated by the Ottomans. The sultans became increasingly more corrupt and inefficient. The Turks had paid a high price for their military adventures by wasting their resources and falling behind the progress being made by other European countries. Little by little the Bulgarians courageously tried to regain their independence. They rebelled against the Turks in the 1590s, the 1680s, and the 1730s, but were crushed each time.

THE NATIONAL REVIVAL

Father Paisii, a monk living on Mount Athos in the Hilendar monastery (in Greece), encouraged a cultural and political awakening. In 1762, he wrote his *Slavo-Bulgarian History*. Then works written in modern Bulgarian began to appear. By the middle of the nineteenth century, fifty Bulgarian schools came into existence, and five Bulgarian printing firms started to turn out materials that opposed the influence and authority of the Greek church. In the years that followed, the independent Bulgarian church began to reestablish itself. Revolutions were taking place in other European countries. The tide of nationalism and devotion to Bulgaria, first and foremost, began to build in the country. Father Paisii had sparked a national revival in Bulgaria.

In the nineteenth century Turkish rule began to decline. The sultans and military officers, deeply worried by the growing Bulgarian nationalism and afraid of losing their luxurious lifestyles, were forced to grant their Bulgarian subjects some moderate reforms. During the Russo-Turkish War of 1828, a Bulgarian peasant liberation movement began, but attempts at driving out the Turks proved futile. By 1876, revolutionary underground units rose in revolt to try to liberate the country.

The patriot credited with planning the armed struggle was Vasil Levski. But in 1873 he was intercepted by the Turkish secret police and hanged in public. Khristo Botev, a great poet, inspired the Bulgarian people to strive for freedom. He was a brave revolutionary leader of a combat detachment. He was killed by a Turkish sniper during a cease-fire. Lyuben Karavelov, another important leader of the Bulgarian national revolution, was one of the first men to advocate an armed struggle against Ottoman rule.

After the uprising of April 1876 failed, about twenty thousand Bulgarians were massacred. Fifty-eight villages and five monasteries were destroyed. When reports of the violence and brutality reached the rest of Europe, many protested. There were

Russian troops enter Veliko Turnovo, which was Bulgaria's capital in the 1870s.

mass demonstrations of compassion for the victims of the Ottoman authorities' barbaric acts. Turkey's grip on Bulgaria had loosened.

RUSSIA AS LIBERATOR

By 1877 Russia had become an enemy of the Ottoman Empire. Interested in gaining influence in the Balkans and with a desire to liberate their Slav and Eastern Orthodox brothers, Russia invaded Bulgaria in April of that year. Heavy fighting resulted on a number of fronts. The most memorable battle took place in the Shipka Pass. The pass was defended by a combined Russo-Bulgarian force of seventy-five hundred pitted against thirty thousand seasoned Turkish troops. A sizable corps of courageous Bulgarian volunteers helped defeat the Turks there and at the Battle of Stara Zagora. The Russians lost fifty-five hundred men in the pass, the Turks, thirteen thousand.

At the Berlin Congress (left), Bulgaria lost territory and Ferdinand (right), a German prince, was named their king.

THE WINDS OF WAR

The Treaty of San Stefano, dictated by Russia and signed on March 3, 1878, set boundaries for an independent Bulgaria. Ink on the signatures on the peace treaty was hardly dry before some European powers, perhaps fearing Russia's entrance into the Balkans, opposed the treaty. At the Berlin Congress, held in July 1878, Bulgaria was carved up into three parts. Territory was lost and more blood was shed before the nation was unified once again in 1885. Thinking that a monarchy would help stabilize the country, a German prince, Ferdinand, who had governed Bulgaria since 1887, was crowned king in 1908. Territories had been in constant dispute in the Balkans since the start of the twentieth century. It seemed that the only way to settle the problem was to go to war. And in the Balkans the slightest incident could trigger fighting, because wars had become so commonplace for that region.

A woodcut shows Bulgarians attacking a Serbian town.

THE BALKAN WARS

The First Balkan War was waged in 1912 by Serbia and Bulgaria against Turkey over Turkey's remaining possessions in Europe. Turkey lost the war and its importance in the Balkans. The Second Balkan War, in 1913, was short but bloody. The question was the ownership of Macedonia. Bulgaria attacked Greece and Serbia, and while its back was turned, Romania advanced against Bulgaria from the north. This time Bulgaria lost more territory to her neighboring countries. At the end of the Balkan Wars, the region of Macedonia was divided up among Serbia, Greece, and Bulgaria.

WORLD WAR I

World War I began in the Balkans. By 1915 Bulgaria became involved on the side of the loser—Germany. The war caused great

Left: Bulgarians served with Germany during World War I.
Right: King Boris III

loss of life and property as well as day-to-day hardships for the
Bulgarian people. Chaos spread throughout Bulgaria, and in the
postwar period the country experienced unemployment, hunger,
and violent struggles between different political groups trying to
offer their own programs for improving the nation's economy and
government. King Ferdinand abdicated his throne in 1918 in favor
of his son King Boris III. Alexander Stamboliysky, the premier,
gave away large land estates to the peasants. After his
assassination in 1923, a reign of terror set in. Thousands of
Communists, workers and peasants, were arrested and brought to
trial. One estimate claims that more than twenty thousand
Bulgarians were shot, hanged, or burned alive during this period.
Georgi Dimitrov became an active young leader of the
Communists at this time.

FASCISM AND COMMUNISM

During the first half of the twentieth century a number of European countries experienced political unrest and upheaval. Power struggles between opposing forces often brought on strikes, riots, acts of violence, civil strife, revolution, and even international warfare. By the 1930s two forms of government came to the forefront. Both advocated economic systems with entirely different philosophies. One was fascism, as found in Germany, and the other was communism, as developed in Russia. Bulgaria, along with other countries at this time, was to be swept up in this bitter rivalry.

Under fascism there was a one-party dictatorship. The government forcibly suppressed opposition and placed private ownership of large enterprises under centralized, highly regulated governmental control. The system was supported by extremists bent on arousing nationalism.

The theory behind communism was based on the ownership of all property by the community as a whole. Eventually it was supposed to lead to a classless and stateless society with equal distribution of goods. Like fascism, it too relied on dictatorial powers, state planning, and decision making by a few powerful government officials. The one-party political makeup emphasized the requirements of the state rather than those of the individual.

THE STRUGGLE AGAINST THE FASCISTS

During the 1930s Adolf Hitler, the *Führer*, or leader, of Nazi Germany, began to expand into weaker states of Europe. He sent secret agents under the guise of tourists and highly trained

In 1941 German tanks entered Sofia.

infiltrators into Bulgaria, which had become a base for German monopolies and pro-German sympathizers. Hitler's tactics made it easy for his army divisions to enter Bulgaria in 1941 during World War II. The government of Bulgaria, already influenced by Fascists, maneuvered the nation into becoming an ally of Germany. It allowed Nazi troops to use Bulgaria as a central base of operations in their offensive war against Yugoslavia and Greece. Bulgaria was interested in regaining lost territories.

In December 1941 Bulgaria declared war on Great Britain and the United States, but refused to participate in the war against the Soviet Union, in which fierce fighting was taking place. Bulgaria was heavily bombed during World War II by warplanes of the Allied Air Command. During the war King Boris III died suddenly, and many questions still remain about the circumstances of his death. Germany's military offensive against the Soviet Union ended with the Germans' staggering defeat at Stalingrad.

The close of World War II left many damaged buildings in Sofia.

Their retreat to Germany was the signal for 250,000 anti-German and antigovernment partisan fighters to rise up against the existing regime. Bulgarians suffered thousands of casualties in their guerrilla warfare against the Nazis and those Bulgarians who had cooperated with the enemy.

The Bulgarian people, while under the control of Fascists and Nazis from 1941 to 1944, refused to turn over Jewish citizens to allow them to be sent to concentration camps for an almost certain death. Not one of its total population of fifty thousand Jews was lost. Bulgarians are proud of that record—and rightly so.

The Soviet Union declared war on Bulgaria on September 5, 1944. The next day, the Fatherland Front, a group of Bulgarian political organizations led by the Communist Party, overthrew the Bulgarian government and joined forces with the Soviets. At the close of World War II, the small country of Bulgaria counted some thirty-two thousand dead, a terrible price to pay and one that would not easily be forgotten.

Georgi Dimitrov nationalized most big enterprises and turned farms into collectives.

THE WINDS OF CHANGE

Soon after the war, a new government was formed under Georgi Dimitrov. The incoming leadership made radical changes in the political and economic practices and began to take the people along the road to socialism. Most of the big enterprises and landholdings were nationalized, put under the government's control. Plans for the country's production and distribution of goods were centralized in state bureaus and ministries. Controls and regulations, made with the approval of Communist Party officials and committees, came from Sofia. Farms and businesses were organized into collectives or run by the state. No one was permitted to hire or use workers for their own individual gain or profit. Sharing of responsibility was stressed. The government would provide housing, public transportation, health care, and free education, and it would assist in providing recreation and

Todor Zhivkov became Bulgaria's head of state in 1954.

rest facilities. There were to be no rich and no poor. It was to be a classless society. All this was eventually to lead to a kind of ideal Communistic system.

New ideas and practices were established, and considerable progress was made in elevating the living standards of the Bulgarian people. The country became more industrialized and there was hardly any unemployment, because all were assured of jobs. Before World War II, 80 percent of the active population was employed in agriculture. In those times Bulgarians were known as "people of the plow." Now, after the war, agriculture, though still important, was no longer the primary way of earning a living in Bulgaria.

Beginning in 1975, Bulgaria's rate of economic growth failed to progress as it had in earlier years under communism. The people's standard of living had declined considerably. Bulgarians became critical of the lack of good-quality consumer goods and spoke openly of the need to have their freedoms extended.

In the mid-1980s under the regime of Todor Zhivkov, Bulgaria's

Turks were expelled from Bulgaria and had to pack up their belongings (left) and wait for their transportation (right).

top Communist leader and head of state since 1954, Bulgaria began a campaign of forced assimilation of the ethnic Turkish minority. Ethnic Turks were forced to adopt Slavic names and were prohibited from practicing the Islamic religion. Relations with Turkey became strained, despite the Bulgarian authorities' claim that the Turks volunteered to assimilate into Bulgarian society.

In 1989 ethnic Turks demonstrated against the assimilation policy. The government began deporting Turkish leaders and prominent Turkish intellectuals. Several thousand ethnic Turks were expelled, most leaving in car caravans for the Turkish border. To solve the "Turkish problem," the government began issuing passports to ethnic Turks who wanted to leave Bulgaria. Between June and mid-August more than 350,000 Bulgarian Turks left. About half of these people have since returned to Bulgaria.

Bulgaria was beginning to look to Moscow and other eastern European capitals for ways of introducing a restructuring of the economy (*perestroika*) and more openness in society (*glasnost*). Demonstrations for change took place during the summer and early fall of 1989. Shortly thereafter Todor Zhivkov was forced to resign from his post.

By early 1990 the establishment of a new, more democratic government in Bulgaria led to high-level talks between Turkish and Bulgarian diplomats. The discussions resulted in a resolution of the problem of the Turkish minority within Bulgaria. Civil and religious rights were restored to the refugees, and most of the Bulgarian Turks that had left the country returned and resumed their normal lives. In 1991 the Bulgarians decreed that the teaching of the Turkish language in the schools be made optional. The political and social changes made in Bulgaria at this time and the guaranteed freedoms written into the new constitution also assured freedoms for the Pomaks, the non-Turkish Bulgarian Muslims, a community of 300,000. They too had suffered discrimination.

In 1990 the Communist Party gave up its monopoly of power and Bulgaria held its first free, multiparty elections in forty-four years. The people and their newly elected officials immediately began to seek new ways to remedy the severe economic problems mounting in the country. Drastic steps needed to be taken to reform the long-established policies of the Communist regime. The country previously known as the People's Republic of Bulgaria was renamed the Republic of Bulgaria, and the Communist symbols of sheaves of grain and a five-pointed red star, along with the state seal, the lion, were removed from the national flag. It now features three horizontal stripes of white, green, and red. A new constitution was written.

Considering nearly thirteen hundred years of violent and

In 1990 a shepherd casts his ballot in free elections

turbulent Bulgarian history, with so many wars, revolutions, and conquerors, it is easy to understand why the people now crave a quiet and peaceful existence. They now live in peace, and that is foremost in their minds. "Conquerors go, but the people remain" is a common saying in eastern Europe. Bulgarians know this well.

GOVERNMENT: THE REPUBLIC OF BULGARIA

The present Bulgarian constitution eliminated most of the arbitrary provisions of the Communist constitution. No longer was national ownership to be an underlying economic foundation of the state. The dominant role of the Bulgarian Communist Party in the decision-making process was removed. The previous constitution declared national resources, industry, transport, and communication systems to be state owned. The national government promoted and protected cooperative associations.

Large privately owned landholdings were not allowed. The central government, under the management of the Communist Party, regulated domestic commerce and foreign trade.

The changes brought about under the new constitution represent fundamental democratic principles. The 1991 constitution declares that Bulgaria is to have a parliamentary form of government with all state power derived from the people. The rule of constitutional law is to be supreme, and individual liberty and freedom are guaranteed. The new Bulgarian constitution also stipulates that citizens must be assured of political and religious freedom.

During the years the Communists were in power such human rights as entitlement to privacy, freedom of movement, expression, assembly, association, or the ability to vote in fair elections often were curtailed. Certain guarantees and rights were mentioned in the old constitution, but they were not always implemented, especially for ethnic minorities and dissenters. The new constitution absolutely prohibits these restrictions. Now the state is committed to the responsibility of providing citizens with basic social welfare and education and is pledged to promote the advancement of culture, science, and health.

The constitution provides for a unicameral, or single, legislative chamber, the National Assembly. This lawmaking body is made up of 240 members who are elected for four years. The laws and resolutions of the National Assembly are binding on all state bodies and citizens.

The president of the republic and the vice-president are elected jointly, directly by the voters, for a term of five years. To be elected, a presidential candidate must receive more than one-half of the votes cast. The president may hold office for only two terms. The Council of Ministers is elected by the National Assembly. It supervises the carrying out of state policy and the state budget, the administration of the country and the armed forces, and the maintenance of law and order. This cabinetlike body is headed by a chairman who coordinates the overall workings of the government.

The judicial branch of government is independent. Individuals and organizations have the right to contest laws and government acts and the right to legal counsel. A Supreme Court reviews cases and has the right to overturn decisions, and a supreme administrative court rules on all challenges to the legality of acts by any branch of government. The chief prosecutor supervises all other prosecutors and sees to it that the law is observed and that penalties are enforced. The supreme judicial council is responsible for reappointments within the ranks of the justices, prosecutors, and investigating magistrates.

The Constitutional Court consists of twelve justices, each serving a single term of nine years. A part of the membership changes every three years. This court interprets the constitution and rules on the legality of laws and decrees, governmental disputes, international agreements, national elections, and impeachments.

Bulgaria is divided into 9 regions, including Sofia, the capital, and 273 municipalities. Each municipality has a council that is directly elected by the local population for a term of four years. The council elects the mayor, who is the chief executive officer. Regional governments are administered by governors appointed by the Council of Ministers who see to it that governmental operations in their territories function properly.

Chapter 3

ECONOMIC REFORMS
AND RESTRUCTURE

In the 1990s, as communism began to wane in Bulgaria, the new government undertook to re-form and restructure the centralized command of the nation's economy. Steps were taken to privatize businesses and introduce free-enterprise policies. Private industry was allowed to operate under freely competitive conditions with a minimum of government control. A market economy, or price system, was established, whereby individuals or firms were free to set their own prices for consumer goods and services, most often based on supply and demand for the product. In January 1993 the new government set up plans to privatize eighty to one hundred enterprises by the end of the year.

In spite of good intentions, more than 90 percent of the Bulgarian economy remained in the hands of the state well into 1994. The two main political parties were unable to agree on the ways and means of implementing private ownership in the country. The even division between the Socialist Party, the successor to the Communist Party, and the Union of Democratic

Forces, despite their commitment to privatization, caused Bulgaria to lag behind other Eastern European nations in economic growth.

In the 1990s, though large numbers of government-run industries remain, self-management of enterprises is encouraged. Companies are allowed to make their own production and sales decisions, raise capital through commercial banks, elect management, and distribute profits as they wish. Many workers are now being paid according to their abilities and the quality and quantity of their work.

Until 1990 Bulgaria relied heavily on trade with the former Soviet Union and other Eastern European countries. The Soviet Union granted favorable assistance to Bulgaria, including low-cost raw materials, technical help, and substantial credits. As late as 1991 more than 43 percent of Bulgaria's export and import trade was with the Soviet Union. By 1993 major financial problems in Russia resulted in an accompanying decline in Bulgaria's economy. Unemployment was high, inflation drastically cut consumer spending, and shortages of basic commodities led to rationing.

Because the Bulgarian people have suffered economic hardships, the new government is determined to seek improved methods of labor production and new technologies. Research is being advanced, and more emphasis is being put on electronics, biotechnology, and chemical industries. Industrial firms that are inefficient are being closed, and labor is being rerouted to more promising enterprises, especially light industry. An increasing number of foreign firms are currently investing in Bulgaria. Joint ventures with foreign businesses are taking place. European banks and international institutions are funding special projects in Bulgaria in an attempt to stimulate and overhaul the economy. A

Many Bulgarians are employed in industries such as the automated machine-tool plant (left) in Sofia and the truck plant (right) in Plovdiv.

major goal for Bulgaria is to increase trade relationships with all of Europe and the rest of the world.

About 40 percent of Bulgarian workers are employed in industry. Twenty-two percent have agricultural jobs. The rest of the labor force is almost equally divided among construction, transportation, trade, education, and public health. One-half of all Bulgarian workers are women.

INDUSTRY COMES OF AGE

In the middle of the twentieth century Bulgarian men and women made products in their homes or in semi-industrial workshops. In 1947 when industry was nationalized, that kind of cottage manufacturing was changed. Today machinery and manufactured goods such as electric trucks, hoists, ships, computers, motors, typewriters, instruments, tools, communication equipment, and clothing are exported to other countries.

Sofia is Bulgaria's major manufacturing city. It produces chemicals, textiles, electronic goods, porcelain, and glassware. Food-processing plants are located here as well. Not far from Sofia, Pernik is known for its iron and steel mills. Unfortunately, like many cities with iron and steel mills, Pernik and its vicinity have a troubling pollution problem. The availability of inexpensive electric power and water has helped the growth of new industries in and around Sofia.

Plovdiv is growing rapidly as an industrial center. Petrochemical plants, cement factories, flour mills, textile enterprises, truck-parts factories, and pulp and paper industries abound. Because Plovdiv is located in the central agricultural area of the country, food-processing industries are especially important. Plovdiv is known for its famous annual International Trade Fair.

Stara Zagora, Sliven, Veliko Turnovo, Pleven, Ruse, Shumen, and Tolbukhin are noted for their food processing, chemicals, clothing, and machine-building plants. Stara Zagora makes fertilizers and has a cigarette factory (Bulgarian cigarettes are in great demand throughout Europe), a brewery, and a giant building-materials industry. Shumen specializes in the assembly of buses. The area around Dimitrovgrad, in south-central Bulgaria, is a new and rapidly developing industrial center. Not too far away, Haskovo's industries include machinery, textiles, and food and beverage productions. Yambol, in southeastern Bulgaria, has similar factories, as does Vidin in the extreme northwest.

Varna, Bulgaria's third-largest city, is an important shipbuilding and dry-dock seaport center on the Black Sea. It has a variety of mills, factories, and food-processing plants. Burgas, south of Varna, has the largest complex of petrochemical works in Bulgaria. It also is the home port of Bulgaria's ocean fishing fleet, so many fish canneries are located here. Burgas has other industries too, including flour mills, the making of railway cars, radiators, cable works, and even pencil manufacturing. Modernized Ruse, Bulgaria's port on the Danube River, produces farm machinery, textiles, clothing, and plastics, and processes food, especially the sugar beets grown on nearby farms. It also has a shipyard.

Bulgaria's largest industrial sector is heavy industry or machine building, which accounts for more than one-fourth of all industrial production. The giant metallurgical combine at Kremikovtsi, fifteen miles (twenty-four kilometers) northeast of Sofia, built in 1963, is one of the largest iron and steel mills in the Balkans.

An industrial problem for Bulgaria is lack of energy. The country produces less than one-third of its needs. And to make the energy shortage even worse, Bulgaria was forced to close two of its oldest nuclear power stations for safety reasons in November 1991.

Bulgaria realizes that its industrial base is aging and needs to be modernized and made more efficient. New technology is being introduced nationwide whenever and wherever feasible.

Left: Shoppers stand in line to buy watermelons.
Right: Women pick ripe green peppers.

AGRICULTURE: FROM PLOWSHARES
TO COOPERATIVE SHARES

In the 1940s, before Bulgaria became the People's Republic and adopted socialistic ways of operating its economy, it was one of the most backward agricultural countries in Europe. Eighty percent of the population depended on farming for their livelihood. If in a particular year there were poor yields or crop failures, the population experienced starvation. But Bulgaria is no longer like that.

Today Bulgaria is like a horn of plenty, overflowing with fruits, flowers, vegetables, grains, and products from farm animals. Roses are grown for their sweet-smelling oil, which is used to make perfume. Now productive farmland covers fifteen million acres (more than six million hectares), or more than half, of Bulgaria. The government once owned most of the arable land used for farming. Although 15 percent of that land was set aside for private cultivation, nearly 30 percent of the total agricultural output came from private plots.

Bulgarian farmers work only five days a week, and often live in comfortable modern farmhouses with up-to-date conveniences. Farmers frequently drive to work in compact cars. When their duties in the fields have ended for the day, they may stop off at the village tavern for a glass or two of the traditional *slivova*, a strong yet smooth Bulgarian plum brandy. Farmers can boast that they earn as much or more than factory workers and can eat meat three or four times a week. At best that was the monthly allotment for farmers of yesteryear.

COLLECTIVE FARMS

At the end of World War II, all land suitable for producing crops, with the exception of little parcels for personal use, was organized into collective, or cooperative, farms. Farmers worked the land together as a group. They were paid in foodstuffs and in *levs* (the lev is the monetary unit of Bulgaria) from the cooperative farm income. This money came from the sale of produce to the government and various market stores and was shared by members of the cooperative. Much of the meat, eggs, fruit, and vegetables produced on the personal holdings of the farmers also was sold to state purchasing organizations.

The Bulgarian government combined agricultural production and food processing with the marketing of the product. These huge enterprises, averaging about 13,000 acres (5,261 hectares) in size, were called agro-industrial complexes. There were almost three hundred of them in Bulgaria. Some of the enterprises did their own canning and even had their own scientists, who were constantly researching ways to improve and increase their specialized farm commodities.

Early in 1991 the Bulgarian Parliament, after realizing that the country's collective farms under Communist management were less efficient than previously thought, voted to restore private farming. Original landowners or their heirs who had had their property seized by the Communists in 1940 had their property returned. Farmers who cultivated collective farms were granted unclaimed land. But Bulgaria did not make a complete break with the past. The state, communities, and cooperatives, according to law, continue to have the right to own land.

Sredets, a short ride outside Sofia, is a famous computerized agro-industrial complex. It covers more than 80,000 acres (more than 32,000 hectares) in size and includes thirty-five separate enterprises in its organization. With its 16,500 cows, 35,000 sheep, and nearly 10,000 workers, its primary responsibility is to produce milk and meat products for the Sofia region. But because Sredets is fully independent, it can sell its surplus anywhere it chooses, even outside the country. Today the workers on farms receive good salaries and benefits and the profits are allowed to remain on the farms. Members decide how to spend the funds that the cooperative earns. Funds may be reinvested in improving facilities or used for constructing new buildings, buying modern equipment, providing medical or educational services, supporting research, or in any other way the workers' council decides.

FARM PRODUCTS

Bulgaria's agricultural production is varied. Many types of grain are grown, but wheat is the most important. Corn is used mostly

A combine harvests wheat (left), Bulgaria's most important grain. Grapes grow well in Bulgaria's fertile valleys (right). Inset: Sunflowers are grown commercially.

as fodder. Barley, rye, beans, and rice are grown, and there has been an increase in the production of industrial crops, including cotton, flax, poppies, hemp, tobacco, and sugar beets.

Sunflowers are grown commercially throughout Bulgaria. The seeds, rich in fat and protein, are fed to poultry and livestock. The seeds often are crushed for edible and industrial oils, and sometimes they are roasted and eaten like peanuts. The entire sunflower plant makes good fodder. The stalks grow from 6 to 10 feet (1.8 to 3 meters) high. It is a refreshing sight to view a field of yellow sunflowers nestling in the foothills of a dark green Bulgarian mountain. Grape growing, as well as vegetable and fruit production, responds well to the fertile soils, drainage, and climate of the Bulgarian valleys.

The relatively small but most diversified agricultural region in the country is in the Maritsa River Valley, between the Balkan and Rhodope Mountains. The cities of Pazardzhik and Plovdiv are farm centers. Subtropical temperatures accompanied by summer rain enable the area farmers to grow almost anything they choose—from apricots to zucchini. The Maritsa Valley could correctly be nicknamed the vegetable bin, the fruit bowl, the breadbasket, or even the florist shop.

Another highly productive farm region can be found in the irrigated and watered fields alongside Route 2, the modern highway that leads south from Sofia to the frontier of Greece. These fields in the Struma River Valley are best known for their vegetable, fruit, and tobacco.

A special feature of the farm regions is the pretty countryside roads. They are frequently lined with roses and other floral plantings and erect, wide trees whose trunks are painted white halfway up. The painting serves two purposes; one is to reflect light for night driving and the other is to prevent insects from destroying the attractive trees. A chemical solution is mixed into the paint to ward off pests.

Throughout Bulgaria the landscape is dotted with vineyards that closely resemble those in the valleys of California. Bulgaria is the world's seventh-largest producer of wine.

Bulgaria is a land of sheep. Animal husbandry is less developed in the country than other forms of agriculture. This is partially owing to the lack of adequate pasturelands. Sheep, which can graze on poorer land, outnumber other farm animals such as pigs and cattle. It is said that there are as many sheep in Bulgaria as there are people. That would mean that there are nearly nine million sheep that need to be watched over by Bulgarian

Sheep (top right) are as numerous as people in Bulgaria. After hay is harvested (left), it is stored to be used for feed for cattle. Calves are raised on a modern farm (bottom right).

shepherds. Their flocks can be seen on the lower slopes of Bulgaria's mountains. The sheep are bred for meat and wool, and the Bulgarians use the milk of the ewe to make their favorite *byalo sirene*, "white cheese," a popular ingredient in preparing Bulgarian cuisine.

Cows' milk is another important farm product. Most of all, few Bulgarians would deny themselves their almost daily portion of yogurt. It is fermented from the milk of cows and goats. Yogurt is considered to be a healthful addition to the Bulgarian diet. Some nutritionists even attribute the reason for the long lives of the Bulgarian mountain folk to their consumption of great quantities of yogurt over the years.

Bulgarians have retained their traditions through the celebration of folk festivals. Food, including bread, plays an important part in these festivities.

Chapter 4

THE PEOPLE: THEIR LIFESTYLES AND CUSTOMS

Approximately nine million people live in Bulgaria. Sixty-five percent of the people live in urban areas. About 86 percent are of Bulgarian ancestry, including some 300,000 Muslims. Of the remainder, about 10 percent are Turks who have lived in Bulgaria for centuries. Gypsies are found throughout Bulgaria and number about 150,000. There are small Armenian, Russian, and Greek minorities. Less than 5,000 Jews remain in Bulgaria.

HOLIDAYS

Public holidays include New Year's Day, National Day of Freedom and Independence (March 3), Easter Monday, Labor Day (May 1), Education Day of Bulgarian Culture, and Christmas (December 25). Years ago it was popular to commemorate these special days with public celebrations and parades. Now it is more commonplace for Bulgarians to observe holidays with family activities and private get-togethers. For the holidays, some still proudly wear their national or regional costumes to add fun to the festivities. Folk dancing and singing at family picnics and home gatherings tend to remain popular ways of celebrating special days.

SPECIAL DAYS

On March 24, Cyril and Methodius Day, Bulgarians honor Saints Cyril and Methodius, educators and creators of the first Slavic alphabet. The day is set aside to show the people's appreciation of the great ninth-century scholars and to demonstrate students' gratitude to all who have contributed to their education. Children usually visit their teachers in their homes and deliver thank-you cards and notes to them. Gifts and flowers often are presented as well. School classes are canceled for two days. Folk dancing, singing, and school decorating are featured. It is also a time for previous graduates to return for five-year class reunions.

June 1 is the time of the year when school classes end and summer vacation begins. The day is celebrated with children enjoying free film shows, puppet theater performances in the parks, concerts, and picnics. Drawing and sports competitions are sponsored, along with other types of amusement. The children usually are taken to the events by special trains, buses, or trucks, each brightly painted for the occasion.

June 2—Martyr's Day—honors the great poet Khristo Botev and other patriots who fought and died in the struggles for Bulgarian freedom. At noon all activities cease. Sirens sound throughout the country, and every citizen is expected to stand at attention for three minutes of silence to honor all of the nation's fallen heroes.

Many Bulgarians are named after Christian saints. On the day designated to pay homage to a particular saint, Bulgarians named after that saint celebrate their "name day." A person named Sofia will celebrate her name day on St. Sofia's Day. Family and friends call on her and give a small party in recognition of the naming.

In 1990, after the fall of communism, a crowd of 150,000 attended Easter mass in Alexander Nevsky Church in Sofia.

Toasts are made and appropriate gifts are presented.

The Bulgarian word for forgiveness is *proshka*. It implies accepting another's apology. Beginning in February it is customary for Bulgarians to set aside a specific day to ask forgiveness for a wrong done to a friend or family member. The person who has caused the hurt feelings or is responsible for some discourteous behavior offers sincere amends. Food, usually chicken, bread, cheese, pastry, and a bottle of wine, is brought to the home as a gesture of goodwill to the offended party. Should the pleas for forgiveness be accepted, the reconciliation is usually sealed by a symbolic kiss on the hand.

Before sunset on the Thursday prior to Good Friday children dye eggs as part of the Easter decorations. Easter bunnies are drawn and put on display. Candles are lit in remembrance of loved ones who have died. Christians go to church on Easter Sunday. Graves are visited and flowers left at the site. The traditional family meal consists of roast lamb as the main course.

An ancient folk custom held from December 25 to New Year's Eve is caroling. Children dressed in folk costumes go from house to house singing songs and wishing good health and well-being to the occupants.

BULGARIAN CUISINE: THE BEST IN THE BALKANS

The Bulgarians have a wonderful saying that attempts to guide the eating habits of their people. They suggest that to be healthy, one should eat breakfast like a king (hearty), lunch like a prince (with moderation), and dinner like a pauper (a light meal). But since Bulgarian food is so deliciously tasty and savory, it becomes difficult to follow the advice.

Bulgarian food consists, for the most part, of Balkan specialties that frequently include national dishes made with lamb, mutton, cheese, and yogurt. Much of what is served may be of Greek or Turkish origin with Bulgarian adaptations. The food is usually gently simmered on a low fire. Bakery and dairy products are available, but fresh vegetables and fruit, both of which are choice in terms of size and quality, are sold only in the summer. Canned fish, meats, and sausages are staple items of the Bulgarian diet.

The Bulgarian *shopska* salad is a mixture of diced fresh tomatoes, cucumbers, peppers, and onions covered with grated white brine cheese and finely chopped parsley. In Bulgaria no meal is complete without soup. *Tarator*, a cold soup, is served in the summer. It is made with yogurt, cucumber bits, and ground walnuts. At other times, soups may be made with beans, vegetables, spinach, lamb, chicken, veal, cheese, or milk bases. Bulgarian soup often is thick and stewlike.

Left: Shopska *salad and a platter of fresh vegetables and sausages* *Right: A food festival, Bulgarian style*

The bountiful Bulgarian table might include other distinctive dishes such as baked eggs with onions; eggplant and peppers stuffed with egg and cheese; a vegetarian stew; baked spinach and cheese; *pecheno sirene*, which is white cheese, butter, and paprika heated in rolled paper; and a popular plate of fried eggs. Vegetables and cheese, appropriately called *mish-mash*; *kebabcheta*, grilled meat rolls; *kavarma*, meat and vegetable casserole; *sarmi*, stuffed grape or cabbage leaves; and *kebab*, marinated meat on a skewer; are well liked. A Bulgarian interpretation of the Greek favorite *moussaka* consists of sliced eggplant and ground meat arranged in layers, covered with a white sauce and cheese, and baked. *Banitsas* are crusty pastries, often made with spinach and cheese. There are various kinds of banitsas, some of which are eaten as a dessert.

Desserts include arrangements of baked apples, assorted sweet flaky banitsas with syrup, and an array of fruits and candies.

Preschoolers work at computers (left) and children take a nap in a nursery school (right) in Sofia.

Turkish coffee, sweet and strong, accompanies dinner for most Bulgarians, but other beverages are served. Beverages might even be a cola drink, but more likely there will be tea, lime and water, or a thick, smelly, gray-colored brew called *boza*. It is made from fermented grain and purchased in big jugs at the food store. And the wines and plum brandies most often are drunk along with a personalized toast, one of which implores all the guests and household members to always be truthful by living up to their word.

EDUCATION FOR ONE AND ALL

It seems that everyone looks after Bulgarian children—parents, grandparents, relatives, neighbors, and, of course, the state. The state's concern starts early. About 80 percent of the country's children aged three to six attend some sort of preschool, generally known as nursery or kindergarten. Some may be taken to the

Left: Students interested in theater attend the
Krustyu Sarafov Drama Institute in Sofia.
Above: The Kliment Ohridski University
in Sofia celebrated its centenary in 1994.

nursery as early as eight months of age under special
circumstances or need. The government allocates large funds for
kindergartens, which are available at low cost for the entire day
for working mothers. Bulgaria has 4,600 kindergartens with more
than 300,000 youngsters enrolled in their programs. Youngsters
must attend school, free of charge, from six to sixteen years of
age. Today Bulgarian students attend general educational,
technical, secondary vocational-technical, and specialized schools.
Some go to boarding schools. Education in Bulgaria is undergoing
change to ensure that students stay abreast of the demands in
science and technology.

When students complete the eighth year, those who pass a
rather difficult examination go to a *gymnasium* (high school) that
has an academic curriculum to prepare students for the university.
Specialized schools stress mathematics, physics, foreign languages,
art, music, and certain sports. They teach students who have
exceptional talents and abilities. Another type of specialized school

offers training in areas such as industry, agriculture, transport, trade, and public health.

Foreign-language instruction starts early in Bulgarian schools, and the study of Russian, English, and German is especially important. The Bulgarian emphasis on high standards of schooling has provided the nation with a 95 percent literacy rate—one of the highest in the world.

HOUSING

In Bulgaria most of the people, perhaps 85 percent, live in privately owned apartments. There is frequently a two- to three-year wait to obtain housing. That is the amount of time it may take to get delivery on an automobile as well. Housing in the cities consists of large complexes of mid- to high-rise apartment buildings, often with shops on the ground floor or nearby. Miniparks, playgrounds, and schools are built to serve the housing units. Apartments are small. Each occupant is allowed about ten feet by ten feet (three meters by three meters) of living space. Lately, however, the per person formula has increased slightly. Each apartment usually has a tiny kitchen. An adjoining balcony is frequently used for storage. Central heating is provided and rent, which can be applied toward the purchase price, is low. Apartment rents are about 6 percent of one worker's monthly salary. Utility costs also are inexpensive. Most city apartment dwellers have refrigerators, washing machines, television sets, and telephones.

In the towns and villages, houses, especially those that are free-standing, are generally larger. Most include individual private plots where vegetables and fruit are grown. Sometimes houses

Many people live in modern high-rise apartments (left) in Sofia. Buildings in the old quarter of Plovdiv have dominant second-story overhangs (right).

under construction remain unfinished for years because of shortages of building supplies. The exteriors of countryside homes usually consist of white stucco surfaces and orange tile roofs. The attractive well-built houses in the higher elevations of Bulgaria are more often than not constructed of wood frames cut or hewn from timber found nearby. Many houses in Bulgaria's southern tier and Black Sea areas have a Mediterranean-style architecture. Some reflect a more traditional Bulgarian or Turkish appearance with their dominant second-story overhangs.

WORK AND LEISURE

Bulgarians normally work from 8:00 A.M. to 5:00 P.M., Monday through Friday. There is usually a break period at midday, which extends beyond lunchtime. Workers in Bulgaria receive a thirty-day paid vacation each year. It is customary for the government

Young people working as street musicians

to allow paid leave for pregnant women, financial assistance for
some children, and limited support after childbirth for those in
need. Many benefits are a carryover from the old welfare system
and are now being reevaluated for costliness.

Health care in Bulgaria is socialized and is mostly free of
charge, except for medicines. There are many outpatient clinics in
the country. Most medical doctors in Bulgaria are women. There is
a shortage of doctors, resulting in overcrowding at the many
dispensaries, outpatient clinics, and hospitals. More Bulgarians are
now using private doctors who charge for their services.

The interests of teenagers are pretty much the same as those of
their peers in other countries. They are becoming fashion-
conscious, go to cafés and discotheques, listen to popular music,
attend theater, watch television, and are avid moviegoers.

Bulgaria ranks seventh in the world in movie attendance per capita. Parties and excursions to the beach and mountains and participation in various sports are high-interest priorities for Bulgaria's adolescents.

Traditionally, few young people in Bulgaria have jobs after school, but that too is changing somewhat. With the end of the highly programmed Communist youth organizations, Bulgarian young people are now free to select their own leisure-time activities without having to contend with the political indoctrinations sponsored by Communist Party officials.

CUSTOMS

Many fascinating customs are practiced in Bulgaria. During the first days of March some people wear pins and give presents made of twined, tasseled red-and-white threads called *martenitsas*. Those who wear them, it is thought, will have good health and have their wishes come true in the coming spring season and beyond.

For the New Year's Day celebration, Father Frost makes his annual visit to family and neighbors. He appears, like Santa Claus, dressed in a red-and-white costume and sporting the familiar long white beard. Accompanied by a female helper, aptly named Snow White, they engage the children in conversations and manage to leave presents in the children's rooms or under the holiday tree.

Bulgarian folktales are popular. Children are especially captivated by their legendary and message-telling mythical elements and surprise endings. Folk songs and folk dancing are

Folk dancers in Koprivshtitsa

still in vogue in Bulgaria and always seem to arouse the spirit of
tradition and nationalism wherever they are performed, whatever
the occasion.

Many Bulgarian village customs center around well-wishing and
hope for a good life in the future. A lavish offering of food on the
New Year holiday table means a fruitful year lies ahead. The
oldest person in attendance at the holiday gathering gets to light
the long-lasting yule oak log, signifying longevity for all. Villagers
tap the backs of friends and neighbors with decorated twigs to
ensure that the new year will bring them good health and
happiness. Christmas carolers wear their regional folk dress and
carry richly carved canes while out serenading.

A traditional village game in Bulgaria was the bear chase. A
shepherd dressed in a bearskin would allow himself to be
captured by a beautiful maiden. The pantomime called for tying
the "bear's" arms and legs together and forcing the "bear" to

Traditional bands (left) use drums and gaydas, *goatskin bagpipes. A young boy with a* gadulka *(right)*

struggle, amid general laughter and teasing, to undo the knots. The playacting symbolized the ancient bear hunts and the power by which innocence can often defeat savagery. The fun-filled impromptu skit was usually accompanied by costumed folk dancers and local musicians playing their *gadulkas*, native folk string instruments; *kavals*, wooden flutes; and *gaydas*, bagpipes made of goatskin.

In west Bulgaria and the Central Balkan Range, young women place their rings, together with oats and barley—the symbols of fertility—in a cauldron of spring water overnight. When they remove their rings on New Year's Eve their fortunes are told as ritual dances are performed. At the beginning of spring masked actors dress up in costumes laden with bells. They act out traditional pantomimes. The bell sounds are intended to drive away evil and sickness. The celebration is festive, like the Mardi Gras revelry found in other countries at this time of the year. On

Folk arts festivals draw huge crowds.

Vine Growers Day peasants prune their vines and sprinkle wine on them before they crown the local "Vine King" with a wreath of vine twigs. On St. George's Day, May 6, young boys decorate farmhouses, barns, and even sheep and cattle with blossoming willow twigs.

CULTURE: LASTING IMPRINTS

Contemporary Bulgarian culture is a mixture of the region's time-honored folk traditions, reflections of its national spirit, and love of country. The golden age of Bulgarian arts occurred during

The National Palace of Culture

the ninth and tenth centuries, when grand Byzantine churches, paintings, and religious objects were created by Bulgarian artists and craftspeople. Magnificent results of that era are evident throughout the land.

Bulgarian literature and arts flourished during the eleventh century, but declined during the period when the Ottoman Turks ruled the country. Once Turkish rule weakened during the 1800s, Bulgarian culture began to revive.

Sofia's National Palace of Culture is the center of Bulgarian cultural life. Today Bulgaria promotes culture through its many community centers and houses of culture. They are supported mainly by trade unions, large industrial enterprises, and municipalities. They contain libraries and reading rooms and encourage amateur arts, song and dance companies, and literature and arts study circles.

This quartet includes shepherd's pipes and a drum.

FOLKLORE AND FOLK MUSIC

Bulgarian folktales tell much about everyday life in the village, certain values and behaviors of village characters, and historical legends—especially dramatic tales about courage. Bulgarians love to use proverbs and sayings in expressing their wisdom and philosophy. Children's folklore blends the best of Bulgarian stories, folk poetry, music, and dance. Bulgarian folk music demonstrates the emotional feelings and moods of the people at certain times and places. The folk instruments most commonly played are the shepherd's pipe (often handmade by the musician), the bagpipe, the *rebec* (a pear-shaped, three-stringed instrument), and a drum. Their sounds set the tempo and rhythm for the performance of group dances and the *horo* (a Bulgarian interpretation of the chain dance) at folk festivals, weddings, and carnivals.

*The stone tower on Shipka Peak (left) commemorates the
soldiers who died during the Russo-Turkish War of Liberation.
Worshipers in the Alexander Nevsky Memorial Church (right)*

ART

A number of imposing monuments have been erected in
Bulgaria in honor of those who died during the Russo-Turkish
War of Liberation. A stone tower rises on top of the legendary
Shipka Peak. In the nation's capital the huge and magnificent
Alexander Nevsky Memorial Church has become the most
distinguished landmark in Bulgaria. It too memorializes those who
fell in battle. It is dedicated to the Russian prince and military
leader, Alexander Nevsky.

In Sofia there is a bronze statue of Alexander II of Russia. He
sits on a horse surrounded by sculptured scenes of the battles that
took place during the war. A representation of the signing of the
San Stefano Peace Treaty in 1878 also appears on the statue. The
memorial is called the Monument to the Liberators, and the
special tribute pays homage to Alexander for helping to free

The artist Christo (left) has created environmental sculptures, such as wrapping the Pont Neuf Bridge (right) in Paris with fabric in 1985.

Bulgaria from tyranny. On the front of the monument stands the inscription: "To the brother-liberators, grateful Bulgaria."

For many years a native Bulgarian has exhibited his talents throughout the world. His visual arts have brought much pride to Bulgaria. Christo (Javacheff), born in Gabrovo in 1935, is a well-known environmental sculptor, a creator of huge outdoor compositions, often made from fabrics and plastics. His works involve hundreds of assistants in their construction.

Christo's art, which tends to arouse strong responses from viewers, has been presented in many parts of the world. He has blocked a Paris street with an "iron curtain" wall of oil drums; suspended a fabric curtain across a valley in Colorado; wrapped buildings, bridges, and monuments in Europe; run fences for dozens of miles in California; and displayed giant umbrellas in Japan.

MUSIC AND THEATER

Bulgarians are fond of music and theater. A number of state opera houses, orchestras, and government-sponsored ballet schools

Folk dancers from the Pirin Mountains (left) and the National Theater in Sofia (right)

are in existence. Folk and dance ensembles are popular, as are the many choral groups that perform throughout the country.

Each year hundreds of concerts are held in Bulgaria. Jazz and pop music have become popular. Ballet always has been a favorite Bulgarian form of artistic movement. Many ballet competitions are held within the country.

The Bulgarian singing group *Le Mystère des Voix Bulgares* is a highly proclaimed chorus, consisting of more than twenty women recruited from all walks of life. Wherever they have toured, their folk songs have been received with great enthusiasm, making them one of the most popular groups in world music today. European music critics have long been enthusiastic about the unique quality of Bulgarian voices in their ancient folk songs. Some have called the sound "fantastic."

Bulgarian opera singers are popular throughout the world. Nikolai Ghiaourov, Nicola Ghiuselev, Raina Kabaivanska, Ghena

Left to right: Poet Khristo Botev, writer Ivan Vazov, and opera singers Nicola Ghiuselev and Raina Kabaivanska

Dimitrova, Anna Tomowa-Sintow, and Boris Christoff are among the best. Christoff, before he died in 1993, was best known for his performances in the Russian opera *Boris Godunov*. Nikolai Ghiaourov was given the Legion of Honor in Paris in 1991.

The popular playwright Anton Douchev's *Time of Parting* is a best-selling work in Bulgaria and abroad. Other popular writers of drama for the theater are Kamen Zidarov and Yordan Radichkov. Bulgaria has a National Theater and many state drama theaters, puppet theaters, and a flourishing motion-picture production industry.

LITERATURE

During the period of Bulgaria's revival and liberation from Ottoman oppression, writings that aroused a national awakening and interest in democracy began to appear. Two of Bulgaria's most appreciated authors of that period were Khristo Botev and Ivan Vazov. Botev's poetry rallied the people against Turkish rule. Vazov gave realistic accounts of the sufferings and heroics in

Under the Yoke. Both of these men used their great talents to inspire a revolutionary fervor and a strong desire for freedom.

Other outstanding Bulgarian writers, novelists, and poets are Elin Pelin, who wrote witty short stories about his native rural province; Yordan Yovkov, an author who described the effects of war; Nikola Vaptsarov, who died a martyr in the anti-Nazi movement; and Elisaveta Belcheva, who wrote under the pen name of Elisaveta Bagryana. A poet, editor, translator, and writer of children's literature, Bagryana expressed her love of life through her writings. Folklore materials were published by George Rakovski. Elias Canetti, a native of Ruse who wrote in German, was the 1981 winner of the Nobel Prize in literature.

In 1992 seventy-year-old Blaga Dimitrova, a dissident and a leading poet, became vice-president of Bulgaria. Dimitrova's priorities on reaching high office in government were directed at improving children's health, cultural policies, and women's status. Much of her writing dealt with those problems, as well as the defense of the right of Bulgaria's Turkish minority to maintain their names and heritage and to be free from expulsion from the country.

HANDICRAFTS

Bulgarian applied arts are highly unusual in that they most often demonstrate long hours of delicate and intricate handwork. Their craftspeople—sometimes skilled peasants—have specialized in working extraordinary embroideries on bedspreads, covers, and clothing (folk costumes in particular). They excel at painting or inlaying small wooden tooled boxes, metal bracelets, necklaces, and belt buckles; shaping wrought iron, copper, and gold;

Left: A metalsmith works on a small copper pitcher.
Right: Intricate lace and embroidery are made in Bulgaria.

ceramics; and wood carving. Bulgarians make vividly colored, locally designed carpets and tufted rugs. Goat hair and oriental rugs are another specialty. Most unusual are the copper bells, carved shepherd's crooks, pottery jugs, bowls, and brandy flasks. And bearing distinguishing Bulgarian trademarks are the small wooden dolls, ceremonial head masks used in regional festivals, ritual loaves of bread, and painted Easter eggs. They have a special flair for making clothing and accessories for costumes.

Over the centuries Bulgarian artists have turned out countless *icons*, small religious images painted on wood using brilliant colors. Many are highly valued, and some are on display in churches and museums as national treasures.

RELIGION

When the Communist Party was the leading force in the lives of Bulgarians, atheism was promoted and church attendance was frowned on. Marriages and other ceremonies that had religious meanings were most often performed in municipal council buildings instead of in churches. Under a new constitution, which took effect on July 13, 1991, the principle of religious freedom has been upheld. Now Bulgarians of all ages may choose to attend church, especially during religious holidays.

The majority of Bulgarians consider themselves to be Christians. The Bulgarian Orthodox religion is the major religious denomination in the country. Muslims make up 13 percent of the population and worship in the many mosques of Bulgaria. By and large it is estimated that approximately 65 percent of all Bulgarians do not practice their religion.

WEDDINGS

Brides wear traditional white wedding gowns and grooms their best business suits. The wedding parties and their immediate families are ushered into an office where they receive instructions and sign documents. The groom's mother pays for the use of the hall, the choir, the official photographer, and the fee for the ceremony. Rings that are exchanged also are purchased by the groom's mother. The bride's parents have little financial responsibility. After the weddings, the parties go to a restaurant for a festive Bulgarian wedding meal accompanied by drinking and dancing. In recent years weddings have been performed in churches.

PHYSICAL EDUCATION AND SPORTS

Physical education and sports were known to the first settlers of present-day Bulgaria in the fourth century B.C. The Thracians were excellent horse riders, and they constructed gymnasiums and facilities for wrestling, gymnastics, chariot races, gladiator fights, and so on. The sports heritage continued with the early Slavs and Bulgarians. The development of the physical education movement became a state policy with the Bulgarian Union for Physical Education and Sports in 1956. Trade unions and other organizations began to arrange all sorts of athletic competitions across the land. Interest in physical fitness and sporting events ran high. By 1983 more than 1,500,000 Bulgarians participated in some form of sports exercises, receiving special badges for their efforts. Thousands of workers were expected to do physical-fitness activities at their places of work. More than 3,000,000 people participated in a *spartakiada*, a kind of national olympics, from 1979 to 1984. Presently nearly 175,000 young people study sports in specialized sports schools and courses.

The Olympics are popular. Bulgaria was one of the thirteen countries to participate in the first modern Olympic Games in Athens, Greece, in 1896. Now there are more than twenty thousand sports facilities in Bulgaria. The most outstanding is the Vasil Levski Stadium in Sofia, but most other major cities have fine indoor and outdoor complexes and sports palaces.

Bulgaria sponsors more than fifty different sports, the most popular being acrobatics, basketball, wrestling, volleyball, rowing, canoeing, track and field events, swimming and diving, and skiing.

Bulgarians have a love affair with soccer, which they call football. Practically every city and village boasts neighborhood playing fields, exciting congregating points for both soccer players and spectators alike. It is Bulgaria's major national sports activity.

Participation is great in gymnastics, shooting, lawn tennis, table

The Maleeva sisters, tennis professionals, are (left to right) Karina, Manuela, and Magdalena. Bulgarian gymnasts (right) are world renowned.

tennis, boxing, fencing, and chess. Eurythmics, the art of performing various bodily movements in rhythm, usually to musical accompaniment, is popular with girls.

Bulgarians are world famous for their medal-winning weight lifters and their record-setting marks at the Olympics. Stefan Botev was the 1987 world heavyweight vice-champion and the 1988 world weight lifting cup winner. Bulgarian weight lifters are known for their sheer physical strength, will-power, and willingness to endure long and tedious workouts.

Bulgarians have won many other kinds of athletic championships, well beyond expectations for such a small country. Bulgaria won ten gold medals at the 1988 Seoul Olympics, ranking seventh out of the 160 participating nations. In the 1992 Summer Olympics, Bulgaria won sixteen medals—three of them gold.

In the late 1980s, Manuela Maleeva was one of the world's top ranked women's professional tennis players. Her two sisters, Karina and Magdalena, also were known in international tennis circles.

Sofia

Kazanluk

Chapter 5

SPECIAL PLACES AND SPECIAL INTERESTS

KAZANLUK, THE VALLEY OF THE ROSES

In the center of Bulgaria lies the Kazanluk Valley, known as the "Valley of the Roses." At the beginning of June, when the roses begin blooming, there is the Festival of Roses celebration. The scent of the roses permeates the air like perfume. The Kazanluk Valley is best known for the damask rose, a fragrant cultivated white or red rose, which is important as a source of *attar* (oil) of roses. The production of rose oil in Kazanluk is thought to have begun about 1580. The best perfumes, made in Paris and New York, are made from the petals of the Kazanluk rose. This is because the oil is especially pungent and has a long-lasting aroma.

Traditionally Kazanluk's women and girls gather the rose petals and place them into baskets tied at their waists. But according to custom, the first rose picked is usually placed in the hair as a decoration. The workers get up at three or four in the morning each spring day to perform this task before sunrise, while the roses are still moist and oily. Before the sun can dry the rose oil in the petals, they are rushed to the perfume distillery. Attar is

Opposite page: When roses are in bloom,
Kazanluk Valley celebrates the Festival of Roses.

exported and used in making cosmetics, soaps, and medicines as well as perfumes. Thirty countries now import Bulgarian rose oil. Two pounds (one kilogram) cost $5,000 on the international market. It is interesting to note that jam can be made from the rose petals, and the flowers are used to make a sweet-tasting pink brandy.

The Rose Festival is a one-day celebration in which a Miss Rosa is selected, and girls and boys wear national costumes decorated with garlands and wreaths of roses. The day ends with an entertaining carnival.

RILA MONASTERY, A NATIONAL TREASURE

In the Middle Ages, with the help of some of the best masons, carpenters, architects, and artists from Italy, Greece, and Constantinople, Bulgarian tsars built churches and monasteries throughout their land. The monasteries were often built in remote places. The monasteries in Bulgaria became teaching centers where people learned to read and write. The monks living in the monasteries frequently produced painted icons. They learned the art of painting religious scenes on wet plaster walls with vivid colors. This technique resulted in murals, or frescoes, that have lasted for centuries. So have the monks' wood carvings and their mosaics of inlaid stones, glass, and tiles. Seven important monasteries remain in Bulgaria.

The Rila Monastery is a magnificent edifice, located about 75 miles (121 kilometers) south of Sofia in a valley of the Rila Mountains, totally surrounded by tall evergreen trees. It was started in A.D. 951 by a holy hermit named Ivan Rilski. Though it has been burned and robbed on several occasions, it was

Opposite page: Rila Monastery, considered a national treasure, houses superb interior frescoes (top inset) and carved altarpieces with painted icons (bottom inset).

repeatedly restored and managed to remain a stronghold of Bulgarian culture and religion, even during the years of Turkish rule. In 1469 the relics of Ivan Rilski were brought to the monastery from Veliko Turnovo, 120 miles (193 kilometers) away, in a great procession. The construction of the present-day buildings started in 1816 with donations from the entire nation. Because the Rila Monastery houses such remarkable pieces of Bulgarian art, coins, carvings, jewelry, and embroidered fabrics, along with thousands of ancient books and manuscripts, it is a national treasure. The United Nations includes the monastery in a list of the world's great cultural heritage sites.

SANDANSKI, A TOWN OF HEALTH

Legend says that Spartacus the slave, leader of a rebellion and an invincible gladiator of ancient Rome, was born in Sandanski. If so, that would be most fitting because Sandanski, a picturesque town 102 miles (164 kilometers) south of Sofia in the foothills of the Pirin Mountains, symbolizes health, courage, and beauty. And it too is devoted to the changing of people's lives. The spartakiada is named after Spartacus.

Sandanski, it is said, has the most ideal climate in all of Bulgaria. It is warm and sunny throughout the year, and the air is pure and clean. Along with its hot mineral waters, Sandanski has a century-old reputation for curing bronchial asthma. Thousands of Europeans who have stayed at its health spas have testified that the treatments they received in Sandanski were effective in curing such ailments as heart, kidney, respiratory, and even skin diseases.

This hotel is part of the health complex at Sandanski.

Patients and vacationers who come to Sandanski for their health, a rest, or a refreshing change of scenery can take advantage of its unspoiled natural surroundings. They can enjoy the calm, quiet tranquility of its nearby meadows, stroll in its parks, or go berry picking in the mountains. For the more active there are always dancing, bowling, boating, hiking, camping, fishing, skiing, and, of course, swimming in either the indoor or outdoor mineral water pools.

Nineteenth-century houses in the city of Koprivshtitsa, where it is common to see horse-drawn carts (inset)

KOPRIVSHTITSA, A FOLKLORE FESTIVAL AND MUSEUM TOWN

Koprivshtitsa is a charming town nestled in the Sredna Gora Mountains, about fifty miles (eighty kilometers) east and a little south of Sofia. Bulgarian folk songs and music played on bagpipes and ancient folk instruments are popular in Koprivshtitsa. Every five years in early August more than ten thousand Bulgarian folk performers demonstrate their rich heritage as part of the exciting National Festival of Folk Dances and Songs.

Koprivshtitsa has historic significance. It claims 388 houses and monuments associated with important events in Bulgarian history.

The uprising against Ottoman rule erupted first in Koprivshtitsa in 1876. A number of rebel poets and leaders lived in the town, where the Bulgarian national spirit ran high.

The village was founded by shepherds, and it is considered fairly new by Bulgarian standards. This town has a melodic running brook that parallels its main road. Some of the narrow, steep roads are constructed of cobblestones and traversed by all kinds of multipurpose vehicles, including horse-drawn carts. A restaurant that serves as a community center for the townspeople is adjacent to the village park and square. Government buildings and a few shops are nearby. The apothecary, a combination drugstore and general store, is almost as popular as the food store. Almost everyone walks, since automobiles are still too expensive for most. Cars can cost as much as five times a worker's annual income.

The solidly built homes are mostly nineteenth-century houses. But in Koprivshtitsa many well-to-do shepherds live in new town houses. The houses usually have at least one upper bay window that juts out over the walkway below. They are made of brick covered by plaster and often are painted in soft pastel colors. Flower boxes laden with bright red geraniums complement the wood beams, balconies, and trim outside the houses. The roofs have broad, low eaves that shade the walls from the direct rays of the hot summer sun. A stone wall with a heavy iron gate is likely to shield the house and protect an inside court or garden.

Inside, the better houses have wood-carved vaulted ceilings, fireplaces for the cold winter nights, and multicolored cushions for the wooden seats lining the walls. Red and blue locally made carpets and rugs cover the floors and walls. Low tables and chairs are used for dining. A samovar for making tea may be on hand, not too far from the well-filled wine rack. Bulgaria produces seventy-seven types of wine, not including the countless homemade varieties that are prepared from "secret" family recipes handed down from generation to generation.

Just outside Koprivshtitsa, off the beaten path, remnants of past village life exist here and there. An occasional water well and out-buildings remain in use. Numerous chickens, ducks, goats, and other farm animals seem to aimlessly roam the narrow dirt roads. But practically every village house, even if in disrepair, has a television antenna fixed to its roof. Villagers throughout Bulgaria now know the world. They tend to simultaneously live with the past and the present.

THE BLACK SEA COAST: SUN, SAND, AND SURF

There are few places in the world that can equal Bulgaria's 225 miles (362 kilometers) of Black Sea coast with its sandy beaches, water sports, and scenery. Because it faces east, the coast is bathed in sunshine throughout the summer. The waters are clean and free of tides or dangerous fish. The temperature of the air is moderated by gentle onshore sea breezes. And best of all, the water temperature is perfect for swimming and the salt content is only one-half the amount found in the Mediterranean. To add to these ideal factors are the green wooded hills, cliffs, and terraces that extend right up to the beaches. Hundreds of thousands of native and foreign vacationers visit from May through October. The Black Sea, with hundreds of fine resort hotels, villas, campsites, and holiday villages, is the main reason why tourism is such an important industry in Bulgaria.

Most Bulgarians, in choosing to spend their leisure time at a

Tourists enjoy the sun and sea at Black Sea resorts.

Black Sea resort, stay at inexpensive holiday houses, often owned
and operated by the trade union to which they belong or the
enterprise where they work. Foreign visitors are mainly attracted
to such seaside meccas as Albena, Balchik, Golden Sands,
Drouzhba, Varna, and Sozopol. Duni, Primorsko, Sunny Beach,
and Elenite also are popular. Each location has something special

St. Sofia Church

to offer its guests, whether it is peace and quiet, a spa experience, a luxurious hotel respite, a chance to camp out, or any number of around-the-clock activities. What they all have in common is lots of sun, sand, and surf.

SOFIA AND HER SISTER CITIES

Sofia, Bulgaria's capital, with its western and central location serves as a kind of springboard for the entire country. At one time it was called *Sredets*, which means center, and indeed it was the cultural center of all of the Balkan Peninsula. After a time, Sredets became known as Sofia because so many peasants began to think in terms of St. Sofia, the great church located there. Originally constructed in the fifth and sixth centuries, the church stands in the heart of the city, not far from its companion landmark, the huge and impressive Alexander Nevsky Memorial Church with its

The bronze statue of Alexander II of Russia stands at the Monument to the Liberators. Alexander Nevsky Memorial Church is in the background. The building on the right with the flag is the Bulgarian National Assembly where Parliament meets.

The fourth-century St. George rotunda

twelve gilt domes, marble floors, magnificent chandeliers, and many remarkable frescoes. St. Sofia is a proud focal point for all Bulgarians and a sight to behold for those who appreciate the finest in art and architecture.

Sofia's motto is most appropriate. It reads "Ever growing, never old!" The city is a harmonious blend of the old and the new. Remains of a second-century fortress wall and the fourth-century St. George rotunda—a striking red brick, domed, round building—deceive one's sense of time. The St. George rotunda stands in the shadow of modern hotels and office buildings and is a short trolley car ride from blocks and blocks of newly constructed high-rise apartments. A mere century or so ago Sofia was a small Turkish town of twenty thousand inhabitants. Now it has a population of more than one million. Approximately one Bulgarian in nine lives in Sofia.

Scenes of Sofia include the UNICEF Memorial (left), representing children around the world, and a busy intersection in the center of the city (right).

Sofia is more than just the governmental center of the nation. It is Bulgaria's chief industrial and commercial city. It is the hub of the country's major cultural life. Its educational roots go back to the fifteenth century. And Sofia is easy to get to, via railway, international highway, or by air, on flights both direct and indirect, from just about every country in the world.

Sofia's coat of arms portrays Tyche, the goddess of chance, protecting the city and wearing a crown representing the city walls. Another section depicts the church of St. Sofia. A third field shows nearby Vitosha Mountain, which rises like a wall over Sofia. The fourth quarter illustrates a small temple to Apollo the healer that symbolizes Sofia's thermal springs, around which the first settlements appeared. The lion, the national emblem, is in the center, and a crown in the shape of a fortress wall is set over the shield. Sofia's motto is written on a ribbon beneath the coat of arms.

Old and new apartment buildings in Sofia have a scenic park view.

For a European city its size, Sofia is distinctive. The old and the new stand shoulder to shoulder, as do reflections of European and Asian influences. A visit to Sofia will leave a traveler with lasting impressions. Such imprints as the beauty of Mount Vitosha as a backdrop to the city and its flower-lined streets, cleaned by stoop-backed women wielding short whisk brooms, will be remembered indefinitely. Also the visitor will be struck by the lack of graffiti and the trams, painted yellow or red, seemingly each having a woman driver at the controls. There will be remembrances of the innumerable pedestrians walking along the roads and on sidewalks toting their plastic shopping bags, the relatively light vehicular traffic, and the historic Ninth of September and Lenin Squares.

PLOVDIV

In the minds and hearts of Plovdiv's residents, their city is first and foremost in terms of pride and heritage. In reality it is

Left: Housing edges both sides of the Maritsa River in Plovdiv.   Right: The Balabanova House in Plovdiv holds a collection of ancient art and furniture.

Bulgaria's second-largest city, Plovdiv is located along the Maritsa River some 80 miles (129 kilometers) southeast of Sofia. Settled five thousand years ago, the early Romans called it *Trimontium*, "three mountains," because of the domination of its three hills. The hills have made Plovdiv one of Bulgaria's most picturesque cities. The same hills formed a kind of cradle for its development.

Much of Old Plovdiv's ancient history is recalled by landmarks that have become popular tourist sites. Remnants of a third- and fourth-century fortress wall offer a breathtaking panoramic view of the entire city. A sixth-century gate is flanked by two watchtowers. A large, three-thousand-seat, marble Roman amphitheater has been restored and is used for open-air theatrical productions and art festivals. Also restored as a remembrance of Plovdiv's cultural past are a sacrificial pyre on which dead bodies were burned in funeral rites, a Roman forum with classic columns and arches, and a stadium once used by daring gladiators. Its

A performance of the opera Aida *at Plovdiv's ancient outdoor theater*

A pedestrian mall in downtown Plovdiv

narrow cobblestone streets and tiny centuries-old shops help one reflect on what trading days must have been like in another time. And the homes of the national revival period show how the people lived here then.

Not all of Plovdiv is a relic of ancient times. It is now a large and flourishing city. New Plovdiv is a major manufacturing city and is at the center of an agricultural and industrial complex. Its commercial past is relived every September when traders from all over the world visit the famous Plovdiv International Fair to learn about and purchase the latest products made in Bulgaria and elsewhere.

The busy port of Varna   Inset: Remains of Varna's Roman baths

VARNA

Varna is situated on the Bay of Varna on the Black Sea. It too is one of the country's oldest settlements. Present-day Varna was founded in the sixth century as an ancient Greek colony by the name of Odessos. But artifacts dating back to the Bronze Age and even earlier have been discovered in the vicinity of Varna. Roman baths of the earliest centuries and Christian basilicas from the first ten centuries A.D. have been uncovered here as well. An ancient rampart of earth that probably surrounded a castle and the ruins of some Bulgarian monasteries have been found in Varna, too.

Though Varna takes on a maritime air, there is a considerable amount of industry, transportation, and tourism. The area around Varna is agricultural, which adds to its economy. The most prominent building on the Varna skyline is the Church of the Holy Virgin. The visitor to the city will be greatly impressed with its modern and attractive pedestrian shopping mall.

RUSE

Ruse, situated on a high bank of the Danube River, has always profited from its location. The river provided a waterway for commerce, especially with the Hapsburg Empire of Austria and Austria-Hungary for more than five hundred years. This is why Ruse resembles cities of middle Europe. Merchant houses and residences are similar to those of Vienna, Prague, and Budapest. At one time Ruse was quite cosmopolitan and many foreign languages were spoken there, but now Bulgarian is the principal language.

Besides being a major industrial city, the port of Ruse is an important freight and passenger terminal. The Friendship Bridge, the largest bridge over the Danube, connects Ruse with Giurgiu, a Romanian city. It has two levels, one for vehicles and one for trains. Ruse has an opera house and a drama theater.

BURGAS

Burgas is Bulgaria's largest seaport. Rail lines feed into it from all parts of the country. It is a gateway city to all southern Black Sea resorts. Burgas once was a Greek fishing town. Fish processing, shipbuilding, and petrochemicals are important industries.

VELIKO TURNOVO

Veliko Turnovo is located in the north central part of the country in the foothills of the Balkan Range. Its setting is magnificent in terms of natural scenery, attracting painters from

The Yantra River flows through Veliko Turnovo (right) and buildings rise up the sides of the city's steep hills (opposite page).

Ruse

Varna

Veliko Turnovo

Sofia
★

Burgas

Plovdiv

all over the world. Situated on the steep sides of a gorge on three hills, the lovely landscape is made more scenic by the Yantra River, which meanders slowly through the city. Along the terraced slopes colorful houses are perched closely, one above the other, hugging the rocks in a near vertical drop from the three-tier cliff top to the riverbank below.

Veliko Turnovo is more than eight hundred years old. It once served as Bulgaria's medieval capital and was important to the country's early history. In 1185 a rebellion against Byzantine rule started here. Behind the hills, on the flatlands, a new planned city with modern conveniences has been constructed. It includes fine

recreational, cultural, and natural places from which to pick. There are caves for exploring, unusual geological formations to admire, mountains for hiking, beaches for swimming, fields for hunting, slopes for skiing, bays for sailing, streams for fishing, and many forests for mushroom and berry searching. There are even places for taking mud baths—for those who like to try something different.

The Belogradchik Rocks of northwestern Bulgaria display likenesses of castles, animals, and people formed by erosion of a limestone cliff. In Melnik, near the Greek border, there are pyramids produced by the weathering of sandstone formations. A stone forest of calcified materials is located just ten miles (sixteen kilometers) west of Varna. There is a nature reserve in the Pirin National Park and a special one at Sreburna, just west of the Danube River town of Silistra, where pelicans and rare birds can be watched.

Throughout Bulgaria, besides its museum towns and historical villages, there are archaeological and ethnographic museums. Many cities have old town sections that trace the roots of occupation back to the early founders. Nesebur, on the Black Sea coast, is an ancient town settled by the Thracians. In Kazanluk there is a tomb with murals dating from the fourth century B.C. that reveals much about Thracian culture. In and around Plovdiv there are numerous sites such as a forum, stadium, fortress wall, and amphitheater—restored as well as remnants—that were built in the second and third centuries A.D. It is quite evident that in Bulgaria there is much to do, see, and learn. There is something for everyone.

Opposite page: Borovets is an international ski resort in the Rila Mountains. Near Varna stands an ancient stone forest of calcified rock columns formed more than fifty-five million years ago (inset).

MAP KEY

Akhtopol	D6	Gigen	B3	Mochuritsa, *river*	C5
Alfatar	B6	Golyam Perelik, *mountain*	D3	Momchilgrad	D4
Arda, *river*	D4, D5	Golyama Kamchiya, *river*	B5, C5, C6	Musala, *mountain*	C2
Ardino	D4	Gorna Oryakhovitsa	C4	Nesebur	C6
Asenovgrad	D3	Gotse Delchev	D2	Nikopol	B3
Aytos	C6	Gramada	B1	Nova Zagora	C4
Balchik	B7	Grudovo	C6	Novi Pazar	B6
Balkan Mountains	B2, C2, C3, C4, C5	Gulyantsi	B3	Obnova	B3
Bansko	D2	Gyueshevo	C1	Omurtag	C5
Batak	D3	Ikhtiman	C2	Opaka	B5
Batak, yazovir, *reservoir*	D3	Iskur, *river*	B2, B3	Orekhovo	B2
Belene	B4	Iskur, yazovir, *reservoir*	C2	Osum, *river*	B3, B4, C3
Belogradchik	B1	Isperikh	B5	Panagyurishte	C3
Berkovitsa	B2	Ivaylovgrad	D5	Pavlikeni	B4
Black Sea	A7, B6, B7, C6, C7, D6, D7	Kaliakra, nos, *cape*	B7	Pazardzhik	C3
Blagoevgrad	D1	Kalofer	C3	Pernik	C1
Bobovdol	C1	Kamchiya, *river*	C6	Peshtera	D3
Borovan	B2	Karlovo	C3	Petrich	D2
Botev, *mountain*	C3	Karnobat	C5	Petrokhanski prokhod, *pass*	B2
Botevgrad	C2	Kavarna	B7	Pirdop	C3
Bratsigovo	D3	Kazanluk	C4	Pirin, *mountains*	D2
Bregovo	A1	Kharmanli	D4	Pleven	B3
Brest	B3	Khaskovo	D4	Plovdiv	C3, D3
Breznik	C1	Klisura	C3	Polski Trumbesh	B4
Brezovo	C4	Knezha	B3	Pomorie	C6
Burgas	C6	Kom, *mountain*	B1, B2	Popintsi	C3
Burgaski zaliv, *bay*	C6	Kostenets	C2	Popovo	B5
Butan	B2	Kotel	C5	Pordim	B3
Byala	B4	Kotlenski prokhod, *pass*	C5	Preslav	C5
Byala	C6	Kozloduy	B2	Provadiya	B6
Byala Slatina	B2	Krichim	D3	Purvomay	D4
Chepelare	D3	Krivodol	B2	Radnevo	C4
Cherni vrukh, *mountain*	C2	Krumovgrad	D4	Radomir	C1
Cherven Bryag	B3	Kubrat	B5	Razgrad	B5
Chirpan	C4	Kula	B1	Razlog	D2
Danube, *river*	A1, A5, A6, B1, B2, B3, B4, B5, B6	Kurdzhali	D4	Rhodope Mountains	D2, D3, D4
Devin	D3	Kyustendil	C1	Rila, *mountains*	D2
Devnya	B6	Lekhchevo	B2	Rilski Manastir, *monastery*	C2, D2
Dimitrovgrad	D4	Levski	B4	Rudozem	D3
Dobrudzhansko Plato, *plateau*	B6, B7	Lisa Planina, *mountains*	C5	Ruen, *mountain*	C1
Dobruja, *historic region*	A6, A7, B6	Lom	B2	Ruse	B4
Dolni Dubnik	B3	Lovech	C3	Samokov	C2
Dolni Lom	B1	Luda Kamchiya, *river*	C5, C6	Sandanski	D2
Drenovets	B1	Ludogorie	B5, B6	Sapareva Banya	C2
Dryanova	C4	Lukovit	B3	Septemvri	C3
Dulovo	B6	Lyubimets	D5	Sevlievo	C4
Durankulak	B7	Madan	D3	Shabla	B7
Dve Mogili	B4	Malko Turnovo	D6	Shipchenski prokhod, *pass*	C4
Elena	C4	Manastir Aladzha, *monastery*	B6	Shumen	B5
Elin Pelin	C2	Maritsa	D4	Silistra	B6
Elkhovo	C5, D5	Maritsa, *river*	C3, C4, D4, D5	Simitli	D1, D2
Emine, nos, *cape*	C6	Medkovets	B2	Sliven	C5
Etropole	C2	Mesta, *river*	D2, D3	Slivnitsa	C1
Gabare	B2	Mezdra	B2	Smolyan	D3
Gabrovo	C4	Michurin	C6	Sofia	C2
General Toshevo	B6	Midzhur, *mountain*	B1	Sozopol	C6
		Mikhaylovgrad	B2	Sredna Gora, *mountains*	C2, C3, C4
		Mikre	C3	Stanke Dimitrov	C2

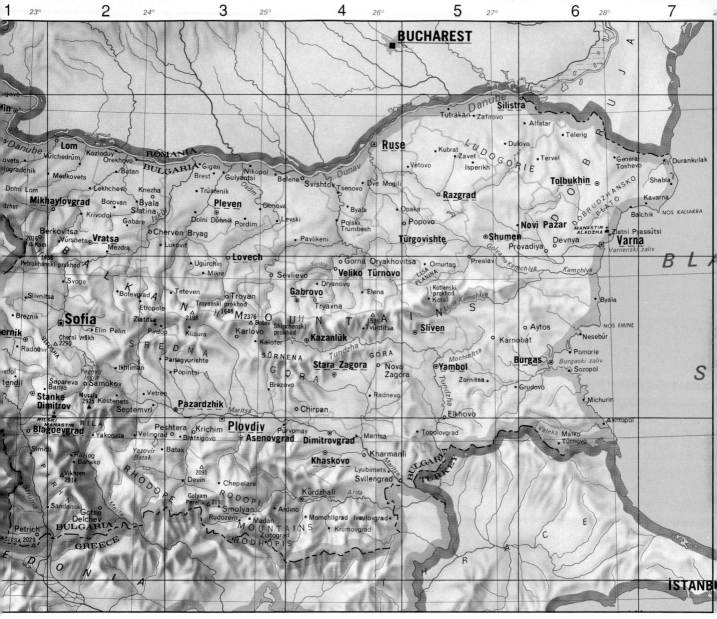

MINI-FACTS AT A GLANCE

GENERAL INFORMATION

Official Name *Republika Bulgaria* (Republic of Bulgaria)

Capital: Sofia

Government: Bulgaria is a unitary multiparty republic with a parliamentary form of government. The single legislative house, the National Assembly, is made up of 240 members elected for a four-year term. The Council of Ministers is elected by the National Assembly. The chairman of the Council of Ministers (premier) is the head of government. The president is the chief of state and is elected directly by voters for a term of five years. The judicial branch of the government is independent. For administrative purpose the country is divided into eight regions, a city commune (Sofia), and 273 municipalities.

Religion: The 1991 constitution does not support any religion, but assures all citizens political and religious freedom. However, the constitution refers to Eastern Orthodoxy as being the "traditional" religion of Bulgaria. The Eastern Orthodox church has the largest following; Islam has the second-largest following. Some 65 percent of all Bulgarians claim they do not practice any religion.

Ethnic Composition: Almost 86 percent of the population is Bulgarian; followed by Turks, 10 percent; Gypsies, 3 percent; and others, 2 percent. There are small Armenian, Russian, and Greek minorities. Pomaks are Bulgarian-speaking Muslims. The Gagauzi of northeastern Bulgaria are a Turkish-speaking group who practice the Eastern Orthodox religion.

Language: Bulgarian is the official language; it is written in the Cyrillic alphabet. Other languages spoken are Turkish and Macedonian.

National Flag: The new flag was introduced in 1991. It consists of three horizontal stripes of white, green, and red.

National Anthem: "Mila Rodino" ("Dear Homeland")

Money: Lev, composed of 100 stotinki, is the official currency. In 1994 one lev was worth $0.015 in United States currency.

Membership in International Organizations: United Nations and many of its specialized agencies

Weights and Measures: The metric system is in force.

Population: 1993, 9,026,000; 211 persons per sq. mi. (81 persons per sq km); 65 percent urban, 35 percent rural

Cities:

Sofia	1,141,142
Plovdiv	379,083
Varna	314,913
Burgas	204,915
Ruse	192,365
Stara Zagora	164,553
Pleven	138,323
Dobrich	115,786
Sliven	112,220
Shumen	110,754

(Population based on 1991 estimates.)

GEOGRAPHY

Border: Bulgaria is located in the Balkan Peninsula in southeastern Europe. Romania is to the north, Serbia and the Republic of Macedonia to the west, Greece and Turkey are to the south, and the Black Sea is to the east.

Coastline: Bulgaria has a 175-mi. (282-km) coastline along the Black Sea.

Land: There is a diversity of landforms throughout the country. The Danubian Plain in the north is the country's most fertile land. The mountainous region comprises about 40 percent of the total area of Bulgaria. The country's average elevation is about 1,570 ft. (479 m). The Balkan Mountains are in the center; the Rhodope Mountains with the highest peaks in the Balkan Peninsula are in the south and southwest. The Black Sea coastal region has extensive stretches of sandy beach. The limestone Belogradchik Rocks in the northwest resemble castles, animals, and people. Bulgaria is subject to earthquakes and landslides.

Highest Point: Musala Peak at 9,596 ft. (2,925 m)

Lowest Point: Sea level

Rivers: The Danube, Maritsa, Iskur, Mesta, Struma, and Yantra are the main rivers. None of the rivers within the country is navigable. The lower Danube River forms the boundary between Bulgaria and Romania in the north. There are numerous lakes and mineral springs.

Forests: Almost one-third of the area is under forest. The chief trees are beech, oak, and pine. The Balkan Mountains are covered by broadleaf forests at lower elevations and by conifers at higher elevations.

Wildlife: Clearing of forests has reduced the amount of wildlife. Historically Bulgarian forests have supported bears, foxes, squirrels, elks, wildcats, and rodents of various types. There is a nature reserve in the Pirin National Park and a special nature reserve at Sreburna where pelicans and rare birds can be seen.

Climate: Bulgaria's temperate climate varies from region to region according to the terrain. The north and northwest sections of the country have a moderately continental climate with warm summers to cold winters. The Black Sea coast has a Mediterranean climate with mild and rainy winters and hot summers. January temperatures are between 32° F (0° C) and 36° F (2° C) in the lowlands but colder in the mountains. July temperatures average about 72° to 75° F (22° to 24° C). The average annual rainfall is about 25 in. (64 cm) but much of that precipitation is in the form of melted snow. Snowfall is low except in the mountain regions. Hailstorms occur between May and August.

Greatest Distance: East to West: 306 mi. (492 km)
North to South: 170 mi. (274 km)

Area: 42,823 sq. mi. (110,912 sq km)

ECONOMY AND INDUSTRY

Agriculture: Almost one-half of the total area is under agriculture. The irrigated fields of the Thracian Plain are known for their fruits, vegetables, and vineyards. The main crops are wheat, corn, barley, rye, beans, rice, grapes, sunflowers, cotton, flax, poppies, hemp, potatoes, flowers, sugar beets, tobacco, tomatoes, and apples. Roses are grown for their sweet-smelling oil. Bulgaria is a land of sheep, which are bred for meat, wool, and milk. Pigs, cattle, chickens, ducks, and goats are raised on farms. Sredets is a computerized agro-industrial complex producing milk and meat.

Mining: Small deposits of iron ore, chrome, manganese, copper, lead, zinc, gold, fireclay, coal, petroleum, and natural gas exist. Nuclear energy provides about one-fourth of the nation's electricity.

Manufacturing: Some 40 percent of Bulgarian workers are employed in industry.

Roughly 90 percent of the Bulgarian economy is still in the hands of the state. The chief manufactured items are cement, steel, electric trucks, ships, computers, fertilizers, cigarettes, paper, perfume, fabrics, porcelain, glassware, beer, wine, canned fish, clothing, typewriters, refrigerators, and television sets. More emphasis is being shifted from heavy industries to light industries such as electronics, biotechnology, and chemical industries. Bulgaria ranks among the top ten wine-producing countries in the world; it produces seventy-seven types of wine.

Transportation: In 1992 the total length of railroads was 4,076 mi. (6,560 km). The total length of roads was 22,943 mi. (36,922 km), of which almost 92 percent was paved. Most of the villages have paved streets. International airports are at Sofia, Varna, and Burgas. The Danube River is Bulgaria's only major inland waterway; it is used for both internal and international traffic. The port of Ruse on the Danube River is a major freight and passenger terminal. Burgas is Bulgaria's largest seaport. The Friendship Bridge, the largest bridge over the Danube, connects Ruse with Giurgiu, a Romanian city. In 1993 Bulgaria and Romania agreed to build two more bridges across the Danube River.

Communication: Bulgaria has about 20 daily newspapers. Television is very popular and TV connections are easily accessible. In the early 1990s there was one radio receiver per 3 persons, one television set per 3 persons, and one telephone per 3 persons.

Trade: The chief imports are machinery and equipment, fuels, minerals and metals, chemical products, rubber, and consumer goods. The major import sources are the Commonwealth of Independent States (CIS), Germany, Greece, Italy, and Ukraine. The chief export items are machinery, food items, and beverages. The major export destinations are the CIS, Germany, Turkey, Italy, Poland, and the United States.

EVERYDAY LIFE

Health: Bulgaria enjoys a socialized health care system with many outpatient clinics in the countryside. Hot mineral waters of numerous spas have a reputation for healing and curing bronchial asthma, heart and kidney ailments, and skin diseases. There are about 312 persons per doctor and about 100 persons per hospital bed. In the early 1990s, life expectancy was 68 years for males and 75 years for females. Infant mortality rate at 16 per 1,000 is low.

Education: Nursery or kindergarten education facilities are utilized by more than three-fourths of three- to six-year-old children. State-operated kindergartens are available at low cost for working mothers. Children must attend school, free of charge, from six to sixteen years of age. After eighth grade, students go to a

Folk dancers demonstrate dances in the Sredna Gora Mountains.

IMPORTANT DATES

4th century B.C.—Alexander the Great conquers the Balkan area

A.D. 600—Turk nomads, known as Bulgars, first enter the territory of present-day Bulgaria

681—The first Bulgarian kingdom is established

862—Cyril and Methodius are sent by the Byzantine emperor to "Greater Moravia"

863—Cyril and Methodius create the Slavic alphabet known as *Glagolitic*

865—Christianity is adopted in Bulgaria

893—The beginning of the golden age of Bulgarian culture

951—Ivan Rilski, a holy hermit, begins construction of the Rila Monastery

1014—Bulgarian Tsar Samuel tries to win back lost territory, but is defeated by the Byzantine emperor Basil II

1018—Bulgaria becomes a province of the Byzantine Empire

1070—The Holy Trinity Monastery is founded at Veliko Turnovo

1185—A rebellion against Byzantine rule starts at Veliko Turnovo

1186—The second Bulgarian kingdom is proclaimed

1207—The siege of Salonika

1218—Tsar Ivan Asen II becomes ruler

1388—The Turks defeat the Serbs

1396—Bulgaria falls under Turkish domination

1469—Relics of Ivan Rilski are brought back to the Rila Monastery in a nationwide procession

1580—The production of rose oil starts in the Kazanluk Valley (Valley of the Roses)

1816—Restoration work starts at the Rila Monastery with donations from the entire nation

1873—Patriot Vasil Levski is hanged in public

1876—Some 20,000 Bulgarians are massacred after the uprising in April

1877—Russo-Bulgarian forces win the Battle of Stara Zagora

1878—Treaty of San Stefano; Berlin Conference divides Bulgaria into three parts

1885—Bulgaria is unified again

1887—Prince Ferdinand becomes ruler of Bulgaria

1896—Bulgaria is one of the 13 countries to participate in the first modern Olympic Games in Athens, Greece

1908—Prince Ferdinand declares complete independence from the Ottoman Empire; assumes title of tsar

1912—The First Balkan War

1913—The Second Balkan War

1915—Bulgaria joins forces with Germany during World War I

1918—King Ferdinand abdicates his throne in favor of his son King Boris III

1919—The Treaty of Neuilly strips Bulgaria of additional territories

1923—An estimated 20,000 Bulgarian Communists are killed

1940—The Communists seize all land from private hands

1941—During World War II German troops enter Bulgaria; Germany uses Bulgaria as a central base of operations against Yugoslavia and Greece; Bulgaria declares war on Great Britain and the United States

1943—Bulgaria defies German orders to deport 50,000 Jews (more than 43,000 Jews survive and finally emigrate to Israel)

1944—The Soviet army helps Bulgaria to drive out Nazi troops

Nicola Ghiuselev (1936-   ), opera singer

Iordan Iovkov (1884-1939), short story writer

Tsar Kaloyan (?-1207), third ruler of Asen dynasty; a shrewd military strategist; established friendly relations with Pope Innocent III in Rome

George Karaslavov (1904-80), playwright and theater artist

Lyuben Stoychev Karavelov (1834-79), writer; leader of the Bulgarian national revolution; edited the revolutionary journal *Svoboda* (1869-72); work includes *Bulgarians of Old* (1867) and many short stories

Raina Kabaivanska, opera singer

Traicho Kostov (1897-1949), an early revolutionary leader; worked for Bulgaria's postwar economic expansion

Khan Krum (?-814), an early Bulgarian ruler (802-814); waged war with the Byzantine Empire; besieged Constantinople (813-814)

Tsanko Lavrenov (1896-1978), artist and art critic

Vasil Levski (1837-73), a patriot who planned an armed struggle against the Turks

Nikolai Liliyev (1885-1960), poet

Manuela Maleeva, professional tennis player

Saint Methodius (825-84), a Christian missionary; brother of Saint Cyril

Anton Mitov (1862-1930), artist

Ivan Mrkvicka (1856-1938), a Czech painter who lived in Bulgaria; founded The Academy of Fine Arts in Sofia

Khan Omurtag (861-931), an early ruler

Father Paisii Hilendarski (1722-?), monk who encouraged a cultural and political awakening in the 1700s; wrote *Slavo-Bulgarian History* (1762)

Elin Pelin (1878-1949), writer; wrote short stories based on regional themes

Ilya Petrov (1903-75), artist; painted scenes and themes of Bulgarian history

Lyubomir Pipkov (1904-74), composer

Yordan Radichkov (1929-   ), prose writer, playwright, film scenarist

George Rakovski (1821-67), folklore writer

Ivan Rilski (c.876-946), a holy hermit; constructed the Rila Monastery

Tsar Samuel (?-1014), a Bulgaria ruler

Tsar Simeon (?-927), called "the Great"; waged war with the Byzantine Empire (894-897); assumed title of tsar (925) of the Romans and Bulgars; educated as a monk, made his court a cultural center; under his rule Bulgaria's golden age of culture flourished

The Church of the Pantocrator in Nesebur

Pencho Slaveikov (1866-1912), writer; son of Petko Slaveikov; his poem *A Song of Blood* recalls the atrocities of the Turks

Petko Slaveikov (1827-95), writer

Petko Stainov (1896-1977), composer

Alexander Stamboliysky (1879-1923), premier during the reign of King Boris III; gave land estates to peasants

Anna Tomowa-Sintow, opera singer

Todor Trayanov (1882-1945), poet

Nikola Vaptsarov (1909-42), author; died in the anti-Nazi movement

Ivan Vazov (1850-1921), writer; wrote *Under the Yoke*

Pancho Vladigerov (1899-1978), composer

King Vladimir, reigned 889 to 893; son of Boris I, and brother of Tsar Simeon; Boris I abdicated throne (889) in Vladimir's favor, but later deposed him in 893 for denouncing Christian beliefs and faith

Yordan Yovkov (1880-1937), author; wrote about the effects of war and Balkan peasant life; work includes *The Harvest* (1920) and *The Farm Near the Border* (1933)

Kamen Zidarov (1902-   ), playwright

Todor Zhivkov (1911-   ), Bulgaria's top Communist leader and head of state during the 1980s

Zahari Zograph (1810-53), artist; famous for secular and realistic paintings

Compiled by Chandrika Kaul

Every five years Koprivshtitsa hosts the National Festival of Folk Dances and Songs.

INDEX

Page numbers that appear in boldface type indicate illustrations

About the Author

Abraham Resnick, a native New Jerseyan, is a noted author and educator specializing in elementary and secondary social studies education. Recently retired, he served for many years as a professor of education at Jersey City State College. He was the Director of the Instructional Materials Center at Rutgers University Graduate School of Education from 1956 to 1968. In 1975, he received that school's Alumni Award for Distinguished Service to Education.

Dr. Resnick has had an outstanding career writing many student-level and professional books. His titles include an array of subjects, including books about countries of the world, maps and globes, American holidays, the Holocaust, the state of New Jersey, and ideas for teachers. He has received two writing awards from the National Council for Geographic Education as well as numerous honors.

The author enlisted in the armed forces during World War II and served as a weatherman in the United States Army Air Corps.

Abe Resnick has a number of diverse interests. He enjoys cooking, watching sporting events, playing golf, bowling, long-distance walking, travel to remote regions of the world, and playing with his five young grandchildren.

Dr. Resnick also has written *Russia: A History to 1917*, *The Union of Soviet Socialist Republics: A Survey from 1917 to 1991*, and *The Commonwealth of Independent States: Russia and the Other Republics* in the Enchantment of the World series.

Dr. Resnick dedicates this book: "To all my longtime Bulgarian 'cousins' who have always made me feel at home in their country. With appreciation and indebtedness for the enriching contributions and special assistance of Katya Milcheva and Jordanka Kotzeva, guides, and Svetla Taskova, translator, during my two field research trips to Bulgaria."